Elijah Wood Meddaugh, Alonzo C. Raymond

The Canadian Railroad Question

ISBN/EAN: 9783744662673

Printed in Europe, USA, Canada, Australia, Japan

Cover: Foto ©ninafisch / pixelio.de

More available books at **www.hansebooks.com**

Elijah Wood Meddaugh, Alonzo C. Raymond

The Canadian Railroad Question

THE CANADIAN RAILROAD QUESTION.

ARGUMENTS AND FACTS

SUBMITTED TO

A COMMITTEE OF THE UNITED STATES SENATE,

BY

E. W. MEDDAUGH, Esq.,

AND

A. C. RAYMOND, Esq.,

AT A HEARING IN DETROIT, MICHIGAN,

MAY 1, 1891.

DETROIT:
John F. Eby & Co., Printers, 65 West Congress Street.
1891.

THE CANADIAN RAILROAD QUESTION

ARGUMENT OF E. W. MEDDAUGH.

The interests of Detroit and the State of Michigan in the subject-matter of your committee's inquiry is very great. This city and State are peculiarly situated. On the east we have Canada and the intervening boundary waters between Canada and the United States. Our only way of ingress and egress from and to the east by railway, save through Canada, is via Toledo, around Lake Erie.

The distance between Detroit and Buffalo by this route, is 361 miles.

The distance between Detroit and Buffalo by the Grand Trunk Railway through Canada, is 259 miles.

This is a difference in favor of the Canadian route for Detroit, and for all Michigan lying north of Detroit, of over 100 miles.

The distance between Port Huron and Buffalo by the Canadian route is 198 miles. This route can accommodate a large section of the State lying north of Detroit. If this section of the State were compelled to seek an outlet east by way of Toledo, the mileage for it would be : Toledo to Buffalo, 296 miles ; Detroit to Toledo, 64 miles ; Port Huron to Detroit, 63 miles ; making a total of 423 miles, as against the route through Canada of 198 miles.

What any obstruction of these Canadian routes would mean for Michigan, sufficiently appears in what I have said.

The Upper Peninsula of the State has its route east across

the Sault river. Shall this be closed? Must that section and the entire northwest be sacrificed to accommodate American trunk line routes south of Lake Erie?

New England, too, is interested largely in this question.

Millions of money have been invested in American railways in New England and the west, which have been constructed with express reference to connection with the Canadian railways, as routes for through traffic between the States. Are these, too, to be sacrificed for the benefit and at the beck of the American trunk line roads? The building of these connecting roads in the United States has been induced, in part, by the established policy of the government of the United States, as expressed in its laws and in treaty with Great Britain, favorable to transportation through Canada.

In addition to the shipping interests of the United States, immediately on the line of of these roads connecting with the Canadian roads, which would be seriously prejudiced by any obstruction to the Canadian route, there is the interest of the general public by all routes. There can be no doubt in the minds of intelligent people of the value of the Canadian roads as moderators of both freight and passenger rates for traffic between the east and the west. It is idle to say, as has been said by some of the American trunk line gentlemen, that the closing of the Canadian routes would not result in higher rates. Competition does its work in the carrying business, as in all other business. We have only to observe what the effect is, on railroad rates, of the opening of navigation each year, to get an idea of the result that would follow the shutting out of the Canadian routes from competition with American roads. The nominal reason urged for Congressional interference with this Canadian railway transportation is the alleged necessity for more thoroughly subjecting the Canadian roads to the Interstate Commerce law. There are two distinct grounds of this supposed necessity: 1st, that the Canadian companies have an advantage over their American competitors in not being bound by the long and short haul clause of the act; and 2d, that being foreign corporations, the Canadian companies are not amenable to process, etc., issued from our courts or from the Commission.

As to the first point: In respect of all United States traffic through Canada, and all traffic between the United States and Canada, and all ocean traffic to and from the United States passing through Canadian Atlantic ports, the law is regarded by the Canadian carriers as applying; and it is observed in every particular quite as fully as it is by the American trunk line roads. Schedules of all rates, etc., on this traffic are regularly filed with the Commission, thus recognizing the law's applicability and requirements. These schedules speak for themselves. Not a pound of freight nor a single passenger coming under either of these classes of traffic, is carried by the Canadian carrier except in connection with an American carrier at the Canadian frontier point. A through line of railway (composed of the Canadian carrier and one or more connecting American roads) exists in connection with this traffic, as in the case of American trunk lines. These lines are, in fact, really American trunk lines with the others, only with the difference that they have a Canadian corporation as one of the links in the chain.

It is evident that this traffic—any part of it in fact—could not be successfully carried by the Canadian railroads, under the existing methods of railway transportation (with, perhaps, the exception of the comparatively small traffic between the United States and Canada, embracing the trade simply between the two countries), without this co-operation of the connecting American roads. And we know, as a fact, that the great mass of even this excepted traffic is carried over American roads on through bills under arrangement for continuous transportation.

Now it is evident to any one who is familiar with the manner in which freight traffic is shipped and carried, that it is not possible for the Canadian carrier to indulge in any practice in disregard of the requirements of the Interstate Commerce Law without the co-operation of its American connection, except in one particular to be hereafter noticed. All traffic between United States points that is carried through Canada originates with an American road, and the contract of carriage is made by it. If rates are not maintained up to the schedule standard, the American carrier is guilty; and this is equally true of all export traffic from the United States via the Canadian seaports, and of traffic carried through Canada to any of the Atlantic ports, as Boston or Portland.

The possible method to which I have referred of the Canadian carrier's violating the law, without the guilty co-operation of its American connecting carrier, in the transportation of traffic through Canada, is by the paying of rebates to the shipper. It is, no doubt, possible for the Canadian carrier, being one railway in a through line, to do this to some extent. But it is equally possible for any American railway company that is part of one of the through trunk lines to do the same thing to an equal extent. The opportunities and facilities are the same in both cases; and the chances of detection are equal.

To make the payment of rebates a success in procuring traffic, while rates continue as low as they have been for the last two years, and still are, all the carriers in a line would have to share in it. No one of them alone could afford to pay it.

The long and short haul clause of the act is strictly complied with by the company I represent, as I presume it is by the Canadian Pacific Company. The schedules of rates covering all of this traffic are regularly filed with the Interstate Commerce Commission. They remain there, open and subject to inspection, not only of the Commissioners, but of the public. No complaint is heard that these schedule rates are not made in strict regard of the long and short haul provision of the law. And no specific charge is made against the Canadian roads of making rates at variance with the schedules filed. Is it unreasonable to ask, in these circumstances, that this ground of complaint be treated as frivolous? General charges of this character are easy to make against the Canadian routes, and they have been poured into the ears of members of Congress and of the public continually for three years past, but no fact in support of them has been stated. We have the right to demand that those who have been so persistently making and publishing the charges now produce some evidence in support of their truth, or henceforth refrain from this cheap method of warfare against these railroad routes.

But it has been said, in connection with this charge, that the Canadian roads are exempt from this clause of the act, in respect to their local Canadian traffic—that is, traffic between points in Canada—and that they have an advantage over the American roads in this. The Interstate Commerce law, of course, does not affect the purely internal traffic of the Canadian roads. Neither does it affect the internal State traffic of the American trunk line roads. In this respect the Canadian and American roads stand on equal footing. For instance, the New York Central Railroad, with its several hundred miles of road within the State of New York, and an exceptionally valuable local State traffic, is, in respect of this traffic, entirely independent of the act of Congress. Neither the long and short haul clause of the law, nor any other provision of it, applies to this traffic : and the Congress has no power to make it apply. The State of New York alone can legislate concerning this traffic. And this is true of the purely single State traffic of all American railroads.

It would seem, therefore, that the privilege of the Canadian roads of making rates on their local Canadian traffic without regard to our law, ought not to cut much figure in this matter.

Still another complaint has been made. It has been said that the Canadian railways have an advantage over their American competitors in being able to recoup their losses on unreasonably low through rates for interstate traffic, by charging the Canadian shipper correspondingly higher rates on local Canadian traffic. The Interstate Commerce Commission lends respectability to this notion by a reference to it in one of its annual reports. (2d Annual Report, p. 69.)

Could anything be more absurd than the idea that our Canadian neighbors would submit to be taxed in this way for the benefit of American shippers, even if the Canadian carriers were disposed to do it? But, aside from this, I am at a loss to see what motive can exist for the Canadian carriers adopting such a policy. Revenue is the object of its being. If what it loses by reduced rates on through traffic it simply makes good by higher local rates in Canada, it gains nothing. The carrier would be quite as well off, to say the least, if it charged higher rates on through business, and did less of it, while maintaining the local rates up to the maximum standard.

But the same conditions exist on the American trunk lines. Each of them has a greater or less extent of road exclusively within a single State, where it has a local traffic not amenable to the act of Congress. The motive equally exists with them to make a high local tariff of charges to compensate them for losses on low through rates. And yet I have never heard of their doing it.

But it is a little strange that in all the talk on this subject, including the report of the Commission to which I have referred, there has been no statement of how the local rates of the Canadian roads compare with the local State rates of the American roads. The information is accessible. The tariff of rates on all these roads is public, and could be readily obtained. Since the report of the Commission to which I have referred was published, Mr. A. C. Raymond has procured the local State tariffs on several roads of the United States, and the local Canadian tariffs of the Canadian roads, and has embodied the result in a printed argument, which, I believe, has been furnished to the Interstate Commerce Committee of the Senate. The result of a comparison of his figures is to show that the local Canadian rates are not higher than the local State rates of the American railroads. This ought effectually to dispose of the charge that the American railroads are under any disadvantage in respect of this matter, in comparison with their Canadian competitors.

What the outside clamorers for additional legislation respecting the Canadian carriers would like, and hope for, no doubt, is a law that will enforce upon these carriers, as a condition of their engaging in the business of interstate carrying, a strict observance of the long and short haul clause in their local Canadian traffic. I will not discuss this. It is too absurd for serious consideration. I think, however, that I may say that the company I represent will voluntarily yield to such terms, whenever they are imposed on the other trunk line roads in respect of their single State traffic. To require this of the Canadian roads, while leaving the American roads free in respect of their single State business, would be a cowardly method of weighting the Canadian carriers, unworthy of our Congress. If it shall ever be deemed good policy to cut off these roads from competition with American railroads, let the purpose be openly avowed, and let the method of its accomplishment be direct and manly, instead of indirect and under false pretenses.

Now, as to the service of process on the Canadian roads, so as to subject them to the jurisdiction of our tribunals in case of violations of the law.

The question that naturally arises is whether the experience of the last four years—the period since the law was enacted—has demonstrated any trouble in this regard? There can be but one answer to this. The American railway companies have not been more prompt to obey any citation from the Commission, or to afford information when called upon, than have the Canadian companies. In no instance have these Canadian carriers failed to submit themselves to the jurisdiction of the Commission in plenary proceedings instituted against them; and they have always given the Commission full information and opportunity for investigation of their methods, etc., when called upon. If my memory is correct, it was the New York Central Railroad Company—an American carrier, and not a Canadian—that refused to disclose to the Commission the facts respecting its issue of passes.

I deny that experience has developed necessity for additional legislation in connection with this point.

If, however, in spite of this experience as to the sufficiency of the law as it stands, Congress, out of deference to this theory,—or for any better reason, if one exists,—concludes to amend the law so as to meet the several complaints respecting the Canadian railroads, I suggest that the amendments should be directed to the alleged evils, instead of trying to cripple the Canadian roads.

The advocates for further legislation openly profess their object to be the subjection of the Canadian railroads to the Interstate Commerce law as completely as the American railroads are subject to it—nothing more. No fair-minded man can object to this. And while I protest that this is fully realized under the law now, there is no reason why additional legislation should not be had in the same direction, if anybody wants it. But the pending bills which provide that the Canadian carrier shall take out a license from the government of the United States to engage in carrying interstate and international traffic, and that this license shall be forfeited as a penalty of any violation of the law, can have but one purpose, and that is to get rid of the Canadian routes. I hazard nothing in the statement that there is not a common carrier in the United States subject to the Interstate Commerce Act, but has violated the act repeatedly—sometimes intentionally—and often through ignorance. This result is inevitable in a system of business as extensive as this is, and which involves the employment of such a large number of agents in its traffic department. Most of these carriers have been before the Commission for this offense, and some of them many times. What would any of them say to a proposition to make forfeiture of their right to continue their business the penalty for a violation of the law? They would probably think it unduly severe, and in this I agree with them. Even if such a penalty were left discretionary with the Commission, it would be objectionable, as vesting in that body a power too liable to abuse under the pressure of great influence. No tribunal, whether judicial or political, should be clothed with such power, except where every other remedy has proved inadequate.

I have to say generally, in respect of these bills and of any and all other legislation that may be proposed, that the Grand Trunk Railway Company will cheerfully acquiesce in and comply with any law that affects all these interstate carriers alike. But why should the penalty of a violation of the law be made different or more in its case than in the case of the New York Central Railroad Company? If forfeiture of the right to carry is necessary and proper as to the one, it must be equally so as to the other. I defy anyone to point out a difference between them, or the circumstances that will justify any discrimination in respect of this matter.

Neither the license nor the added penalty would remove the alleged facility of the carrier in Canada for disregarding the law, nor would either aid in detecting such violations when they occur. This must be apparent to anyone. And yet the opportunity of the Canadian roads for fraud upon the act, and the difficulty of detecting them in it, was gravely urged by the gentleman who suggested this license legislation, as the reason for it.

If it is simply desired to place the Canadian railway companies in the same position as the carriers in the States, respecting the service of process on them, obedience to final orders, etc.—whether of the Commission or of the courts— and all inquisitorial rights with which the Commission is clothed, here is an opportunity for use of the forfeiture power. Amend the act of Congress so as to impose a penalty of forfeiture of the right to continue the interstate business, upon all carriers that are subject to the act, for failure to obey process served upon them, whether served within the United States or in an adjacent foreign country, or to subject themselves to the jurisdiction of the Commission or court from which it issues. And impose a like penalty for refusal or neglect to obey final orders or decrees, or to satisfy final judgment, saving always the right of appeal; and for refusal or neglect to yield to the Commission in the exercise of its inquisitorial powers.

If the American railroad gentlemen are honest in the profession of what they want to accomplish, such an amendment of the law will be satisfactory to them.

One of the bills now pending in Congress requires these Canadian carriers to give a bond to the United States government for obedience to the law. The legislation I suggest would be much more effective than a bond, as the remedy would be direct in each case of violation.

But, in fairness, the law should apply to all alike. There is no excuse for making in this matter two rules—one for the Canadian roads, and a different one, less stringent, for the American roads.

If the only interests involved were those of the trunk line railway companies south of Lake Erie, as against the Canadian roads, a narrow and illiberal national policy might favor any legislation to cripple the Canadian roads. But this is not the case. There are, in the first place, large systems of railway in the United States, representing in the cost of construction a great many millions of dollars, the prosperity—indeed, the very life of which—depends upon the uninterrupted course of interstate traffic through Canada; and the Congress of the United States is bound not to do anything, save from national necessity, to the injury of these systems of railway; and surely the desire of these trunk line roads to get rid of Canadian railway competition can hardly form the basis of such national action. It will not do to sacrifice this great American interest for the benefit of the American trunk line railways.

But these American railway interests, which are so inextricably bound up with the Canadian roads, are not all, even if they are the greater, American interests to be prejudicially affected by a disturbance of the Canadian routes. As I have already intimated in the opening of this discussion, there is the shipping public of all New England, on the east, and of a dozen great States in the west and northwest. If the shippers in these States—the producer, the merchant and the manufacturer, have no interest in this question, it is pretty evident that they think they have. For they have given utterance to most vigorous protests, within the last two years, through boards of trade and other commercial organizations, against any action by our government that might have the effect to impair the efficiency of these Canadian routes of transportation for United States traffic. It would not be a difficult task, I believe, to show that they do not overestimate the value of these routes to the sections of the United States for which they speak. But I will not occupy time for this. There is a presumption that such bodies of intelligent American citizens are the best judges of their own interests in such a question. This aspect of it can be safely left to them.

The Grand Trunk Railway is one section only of a great American trunk line route extending from Chicago to the Atlantic seaboard points of New York, Boston and Portland. Between Chicago and New York, a distance by its route of 942 miles, there is only 196 miles of the transportation on Canadian territory. All the rest is in the United States and over the railroads of American corporations. Between Chicago and Boston, a distance by this route of 1184 miles, 557 miles of the transportation is in Canada, and the remainder is in the United States, and on railroads of American corporations. Between Chicago and Portland, a distance of 1136 miles, there is transportation in Canada of 650 miles, and the remainder is in the United States, and on American railroads.

These American railroads, profoundly interested in the continuance of this route through Canada unembarrassed by obstructive legislation, represent in the aggregate a capital investment of $85,000,000.

No words of mine can add anything to the eloquent appeal of this statement against the kind of legislation that Congress has been asked for on this subject.

The Grand Trunk Railway Company has another American feature that entitles it to some consideration. It has constructed and promoted the construction of, and has a very large pecuniary interest in, more than 1,000 miles of railroad in the United States. Its capital investment in these railroads, every one of which is an American corporation, amounts to many millions of dollars.

It is generally well known that the established method among railway companies forming a continuous line for carrying freight is by the creation of what is known as fast freight lines. These lines are established by agreement of the companies composing them, each contributing its quota of cars, on an agreed basis, for use in the business of the line. It shows something of the extent of the Grand Trunk Railway Company's traffic arrangements with its American railway connections, that it is a party in the following fast freight lines, under agreements with the American railway companies named:

The Michigan & Milwaukee Fast Freight Line, in connection with the New York Central Railroad Co.

The Commercial Express Line, in connection with the New York, Lake Erie & Western Railroad Co.

The Hoosac Tunnel Line, in connection with the West Shore & Fitchburg Railroads.

The Great Eastern Fast Freight Line, in connection with the Delaware, Lackawanna & Western Railroad Co. and the Central Vermont Railroad Co.

The Wabash & Lehigh Valley Fast Freight Line, in connection with the Lehigh Valley Railroad Co.

The Ontario Despatch Line, in connection with the New York, Ontario & Western Railroad Co.

The National Despatch Line, in connection with the Central Vermont R. R., and its connections at White River Junction for New England points.

This company has also a through passenger service in connection with the West Shore Railroad Co., of which the New York Central Railroad Co. is lessee, and with the New York, Lake Erie & Western R. R. Co. The Grand Trunk road is, in fact, the recognized and established westtern connection of the West Shore road for both passengers and freight.

No one familiar with the railways from New York City centering at Buffalo, will fail to appreciate at once what the effect would be upon them, if they were deprived of the route through Canada by the Grand Trunk road as a feeder to them of interstate traffic. The New York Central alone would gain by it. The others would suffer great loss.

In addition to all its railroad investments in the United States, the Grand Trunk Company has just completed the construction of an international railroad tunnel between Port Huron and Sarnia, under the River St. Clair, at a cost of about $3,000,000. Possibly, however, some timid souls in the United States may see lurking in all this a deep-laid plan on the part of this corporation, in co-operation with the Canadian government, to afford greater facilities to the Canadian government for moving an army of conquest against us from that country.

In the face of these facts, is it not apparent that any action by the government of the United States by the imposition of burdens on the Grand Trunk Railway Company in connection with this interstate traffic, that are not imposed upon the exclusively American trunk lines, would result in a serious injury to other large American railway interests, and to the interests of a large section of American producers, merchants and manufacturers? These aggregate interests are much too large and important to be sacrificed for the benefit of any other interest, either railway or sectional.

There are many other considerations which have a bearing on this Canadian railway transportation question, that I should like to discuss, and only refrain from discussing them here for fear of consuming more time than justly belongs to me, and possibly trespassing on the patience of the committee.

The demand of the American public everywhere is continually heard in all sections for cheap and still cheaper rates of transportation. In this direction lies the hope for greater prosperity in all departments of business. The difference of a few cents on a hundred in the transportation of grain from the rich fields of its production in the west, to the Atlantic seaboard, determines the possibility of its being profitably marketed abroad. And this is true of all our vast surplus of production of every kind. The United States, therefore, cannot afford to close any route now open to it that cheapens the rates of transportation between the places of production and the market. These routes through Canada unquestionably have this effect. This is the invariable testimony of every shipping centre tributary to these routes. It may, with equal show of reason, be contended that the waterways of the great lakes do not have a reducing effect on rates, during the season of navigation, as that these Canadian railway routes are ineffective in this respect.

The foregoing is the substance of my remarks submitted to the special committee of the United States Senate. Messrs. Henry Russel and Ashley Pond, representing the Michigan Central R. R. Co., followed me on the occasion. Reference was made by them to the percentage of the east bound traffic out of Chicago taken by the Canadian rail routes, which was claimed to be excessive as against the exclusively American routes; and the inference was indulged in and urged that such a percentage of the business could only be secured for the Canadian routes by the payment of rebates. And the alleged difficulty of investigating the Canadian railway companies in respect of such rebate payments was urged as a reason for so amending the law as to require these corporations to obtain a license for engaging in interstate traffic and imposing a forfeiture of the license as a penalty for violations of the law.

Now, if these gentlemen honestly believe that rebates are being so paid, they owe it to the carrier they represent, if not to the public, to call attention of the Interstate Commerce Commission to the fact, and ask an investigation. Why do they not try this method of redress, instead of airing their suspicions before a Committee of the Senate? Here is a good opportunity to demonstrate any defects in the law and the alleged practical difficulties in the way of an official investigation of the practices of the Canadian railways. But it was further said that this undue percentage of the Chicago traffic taken by the Canadian roads was mostly confined to dressed beef shipments, and that this enormous business is in the hands of less than half a dozen of well-known shippers of beef—which is a fact; and it was assumed that rebates are being paid to these few shippers. If there is any foundation in fact for this assumption, these shippers are equally guilty, under the law, with the carrier that pays the rebate; and they should be punished. What stands in the way of an investigation of this subject in respect of them? They are all American residents, and have their places of business in the United States. Their account books, papers, etc., can be examined. They are amenable to process from the Interstate Commerce Commission and from the United States courts. Why have not these railway gentlemen, so burdened with suspicions of fraud, promoted a judicial inquiry into the facts? They have not the poor excuse here, that they offer in connection with the Canadian railroads, that the parties are in foreign territory.

With American shippers as necessarily guilty parties to any alleged system of rebate payments by the Canadian carriers, and with these carriers openly declaring their willingness to submit themselves, and all books, accounts, papers, etc., to the inspection of the Commission or court, in any proceeding that may be instituted for an investigation of the facts, the gentlemen who make these gratuitous charges, based solely on their suspicions, in neglecting to take the responsibility of moving, in the way plainly pointed out by the law, for an investigation, lay themselves open to the grave suspicion of not really believing what they profess to believe in this matter.

There is an offensive assumption of superior virtue on the

part of these gentlemen, involved in their charges as made against these carriers. They assume that the Canadian railway officers and traffic agents are not above resorting to devices for evading the law's requirements, which are equally open to any one of the railways in the United States, but which the officers and agents of the latter are morally above having recourse to as a means of securing traffic. They would experience some difficulty, I think, in establishing this as a fact in the minds of American shippers who have had many years of experience in shipping by the different routes. "Comparisons are odious," but the officers and traffic agents of the Canadian railways have no reason to shrink from comparison in this connection. They are not unknown to the commercial men in the United States; and I do not hesitate to make the assertion that, taken together, they stand quite as high for manly integrity in all business relations as the officers and agents of any American railway corporation. The American shipping public will be slow to believe that these Canadian railway companies, in order to get traffic, have resorted to methods of violating the law that are equally open to the officers and agents of their American competitors, but which the latter have proved too honest to adopt.

If rebates have been paid for traffic by the Canadian railways, I neither know nor have heard of any instance of the kind. The point I made, and wish here to emphasize, is simply that it is no more liable to be done by the carriers on these routes than by the carriers on any of the routes exclusively within the United States; that the facilities for doing it are no greater by the one route than by the other; and that the opportunities for detection are the same by all routes. Whatever may be done in evasion of the law by the Grand Trunk Railway Co., for instance, in connection with any traffic it may carry—whether it be the payment of rebates or anything else—may also be done, and with no greater risk, by any one of the trunk line railway companies; and furthermore, is quite as liable, to say the least, to be done by one of the latter as by the former.

I do not feel justified in adding much to what I said to the Committee in opening the discussion, on the subject of requiring the Canadian railroads to take out a license for engaging in the interstate traffic business. I then pointed out that such a license would not in the slightest degree remove the alleged difficulty of detecting violations of the law by the Canadian carriers, and that the penalty of forfeiture of the license for any violation was too severe, and fraught with danger from its susceptibility to abuse. I further urged that such license should not be required of the Canadian carrier, unless required also of the American carrier; that there is no good ground for such discrimination.

It was said by Messrs. Russel and Pond, in reply, that if the license were required, and the penalty of forfeiture existed, it would have the effect of making the Canadian carrier more careful in observing the Interstate Commerce law. If this is true as to these carriers, would not the effect of such a license system be equally wholesome for the American carriers, and should it not, therefore, be extended to them? If the reasoning is worth anything, it goes to this extent. As I have said, there is no basis in reason for a distinction in this matter between these railroads.

But no account is taken by the promoters of this license scheme with forfeiture, of the consequences to the carrier and the public of a temporary suspension of business on one of these routes—a suspension, say, of ninety days. In the first place, the carrier could not recover its business after such a suspension, for many months. The loss would be irreparable. Shippers by its route would have entered into arrangements more or less permanent with other routes. It would be extremely difficult, and take a long time, to recover the amount of traffic thus lost.

The embarrassing effect on the public, accustomed to rely on the particular route, would also be very great. Even that part of the public immediately tributary to it, and which might be specially accommodated by it, would be forced to seek another and more remote route of shipment, involving for them, not only much inconvenience, but a large additional expense.

This is only hinting at some of the consequences that would follow the forfeiture of a license, for even a brief period of time. There are many other and very serious results that would inevitably ensue, which will readily occur to any one who thinks the matter out. The penalty is too severe, in addition to the fact that it would inflict punishment on the innocent. The idea, I submit, is not creditable to its inventor. All the benefits combined of the Interstate Commerce law are not worth this cost.

In correction of the statement made by Mr. Russel as to the percentage of the aggregate of east-bound traffic out of Chicago which has been taken by the Canadian routes, I submit the following tables, showing:

1. The total shipments of live stock during the year 1890 and the first three months of 1891, and the percentage carried by each route.

2. A similar statement in respect of the dressed beef.

3. A similar statement in respect of all other traffic.

These statements are taken from the official record of the Central Traffic Association, and are therefore reliable.

The last statement does not include the Wabash, the Chicago & Erie, or the C. C. C. & St. L. lines, for the reason that no reports have been made by them, and it is impossible to give the figures.

Live Stock Shipments from Chicago.

ROADS.	Year 1890.		Jan, Feb., March, 1891.	
	Tons.	Per Cent.	Tons.	Per Cent.
C. & G. T.	233,274	22.4	57,097	18.8
M. C.	114,823	11.0	23,851	7.8
L. S. & M. S.	196,519	18.9	84,067	27.6
P. F. W. & C.	186,796	18.0	48,888	16.1
P. C. C. & St. L.	16,848	1.6	4,266	1.4
B. & O.	84,232	8.1	25,735	8.5
N. Y. C. & St. L.	198,753	19.1	52,660	17.3
C. & Erie.	7,112	0.7	7,087	2.3
Wabash	1,815	0.2	412	0.2
C. C. C. & St. L.	......	....	......	....
Total	1,040,172	100.0	304,063	100.0

Dressed Beef Shipments from Chicago.

ROADS.	Year 1890.		Jan, Feb., March, 1891.	
	Tons.	Per Cent.	Tons.	Per Cent.
C. & G. T.	134,999	22.5	29,794	22.8
M. C.	133,334	22.3	39,854	30.5
L. S. & M. S.	115,628	19.3	15,200	11.6
P. F. W. & C.	31,019	5.2	5,629	4.3
P. C. C. & St. L.	56,248	9.4	11,528	8.8
B. & O.	21,042	3.5	6,050	4.6
N. Y. C. & St. L.	5,465	0.9	1,258	1.0
C. & Erie.	15,569	2.6	2,116	1.6
Wabash	84,107	14.0	18,520	14.2
C. C. C. & St. L.	1,912	0.3	896	0.6
Total	599,323	100.0	130,845	100.0

Dead Freight Tonnage from Chicago.

ROADS.	Year 1890.		Jan., Feb., March, 1891.	
	Tons.	Per Cent.	Tons.	Per Cent.
B. & O.	445,266	14.5	101,205	13.1
C. & G. T.	475,582	15.5	165,650	21.3
P. C. C. & St. L.	206,092	6.7	39,026	5.0
L. S. & M. S.	512,355	16.7	115,722	14.8
M. C.	512,125	16.7	125,699	16.1
N. Y. C. & St. L.	384,786	12.6	117,016	15.1
P. F. W. & C.	530,254	17.3	113,763	14.6
Total	3,066,460	100.0	778,081	100.0

These official statements carry their own refutation of the extravagant figures named by Mr. Russel as the percentage of the Chicago east-bound traffic which had been taken by the Canadian routes. Comment is unnecessary.

But I desire in this connection to invite attention to the

percentages of this traffic shown by these statements to have been carried by some of the other routes. For the year 1890 the Lake Shore road, in connection with the New York Central, carried of the live stock 18 per cent and a fraction ; and for the three first months of 1891 it carried 27 per cent and a fraction ; while the Michigan Central R. R. carried, for the corresponding periods respectively, 11 per cent and 7.8 per cent. According to Mr. Pond's logic the Lake Shore & Michigan Southern Company must have been paying rebates to secure this undue percentage over the Michigan Central Company. The route of the latter from Chicago to Buffalo is quite equal to that of the Lake Shore Company, and the shorter as a matter of fact ; and from Buffalo east the route is the same for both.

During the same period the Michigan Central Railroad carried 22 per cent and a fraction of the dressed beef in the year, and 30 per cent and a fraction in the three months of 1891, as against 19 per cent and a fraction carried by the Lake Shore & Michigan Southern road for the year, and 11 per cent and a fraction for the three months. Is it possible that the Michigan Central Railroad Company was paying rebates on this traffic ? The inference is not only legitimate, but it is irresistible, according to Mr. Pond.

Now in respect of the percentages of this Chicago traffic east-bound, I contend that the Michigan Central and Lake Shore Railroads should not be treated fully as two separate and equal factors as against the Chicago & Grand Trunk Railway. The latter has not only its New England connections, but it has several railroads at Buffalo connecting with New York, all of which want a share of this Chicago traffic, and in fairness have a right to it equally with the New York Central Railroad. The Michigan Central and Lake Shore roads are simply feeders of the New York Central road, as to the great bulk of this traffic carried by them. The situation therefore, I submit, does not justify each of these in the demand for an equal percentage of this traffic with the Chicago & Grand Trunk Railway Company.

In conclusion, I deny that the Canadian routes have taken an undue proportion of the Chicago east-bound traffic. What they have got, they have, I believe, secured by legitimate business methods, and without violating the law. Courtesy and a spirit of accommodation are as potent in this department of business as in any other. A good deal of the popular favor which the Grand Trunk Railway Company enjoys and reaps benefit from with the shipping public of the United States, is no doubt due to the civility of its officers and agents. There is more virtue in this as an agency for getting traffic than has yet been dreamed of by some of our American railway friends.

THE CANADIAN RAILROAD QUESTION

ARGUMENT OF A. C. RAYMOND.

Mr. Chairman—It is now a little more than two years since the agitation of the Canadian railway question began in the Congress of the United States. For more than fifteen years the competition between American and Canadian railways has been continuous and bitter, and next to the lake and canal route from the West to the sea-board, the Canadian railways have exercised the most controlling regulative influence upon rates of transportation. From this competition American merchants, shippers, producers and consumers have received inestimable benefits. Large areas of American territory, notably New England and the West and Northwest, have been put in communication with each other at such advantageous rates for transportation as had not been made and indeed could not be made over purely American lines. Nearly all those portions of interior New England lying north of the Boston & Albany Railroad, were formerly compelled to pay by the addition of what is known as "arbitraries," much higher rates than those current to Boston. The advent of the Grand Trunk Railway of Canada largely swept away these "arbitraries," and placed all portions of New England upon substantially the Boston basis. Many and relentless were the attacks upon the Grand Trunk Railway by its American competitors, but although sorely bruised and beaten in the conflict it has always steadily held every field of which it has once possessed itself. With the exception of occasional periods of peace and compromise, this state of warfare was well nigh continuous up to the time of the passage of the Interstate Commerce Act which took effect April 5th, 1887.

The novel sensation of national control, and the new adjustments thereby rendered necessary, diverted the attention of the American railways from their old competitor for nearly a year. The American lines discovering that the Interstate Commerce Act had not bankrupted them, as they had so confidently asserted pending its passage, but that their traffic was enlarging and their revenues were increasing, began to seek for new means of chastening their imperturbable Canadian rival. The former rough and forceful methods of ruinous competition were rendered obsolete by the Interstate Commerce Act, but an ingenious and, if successful, far more effective one, remained. It was to transfer to the halls of Congress, the contest heretofore so fiercely waged in the field, and to appeal to the patriotic instincts of the American people to shield their infant (?) railroad industries from impending destruction at the hands of menacing foreign corporations.

The preliminary skirmishing promptly began under the leadership of that dashing cavalryman of the late civil war, General J. H. Wilson, of Wilmington, Delaware, who appeared at Washington before the Senate Committee of Interstate Commerce February 10th, 1888, and made an elaborate attack upon Canadian railways. March 16th, 1888, he repeated this attack by a long speech before the Committee on Commerce of the House of Representatives, in which he advocated the exclusion of Canadian railways from participation in American traffic, and the abolition of the "Transit in Bond system" which had been in continuous operation since it was authorized by Act of Congress in 1866. Especial prominence was given to these speeches by a certain leading American journal which published them in full, and in vigorous leading articles at frequent intervals, promoted and advocated Wilson's scheme. A set of resolutions embodying it was promptly introduced into the House of Representatives and referred to the Committee on Commerce. Thus was "the leaven hid in the measure of meal."

Instant and overwhelming protests were made by the various commercial organizations in Portland, Boston, Detroit, Chicago, Milwaukee, Minneapolis, St. Paul, Duluth and Peoria. The newspapers in these cities with one voice denounced the proposed destruction of the competition of the Canadian lines, and petitions, remonstrances and memorials, came pouring into Congress in a flood, and the House Committee on Commerce took no action on the resolutions.

The subject was revived in the 50th Congress by an amendment to the Senate Tariff Bill, proposed by Senator Morgan, of Alabama, to the effect of prohibiting the importation in bond through American sea-ports, of merchandise designed for Canadian markets. This was, however, defeated. Meanwhile the American competing interests had not been idle, but through the columns of the press and otherwise, continued industriously and unceasingly to complain of the ravages of the foreign railway corporations, which resulted in Congress authorizing the Senate Committee on Interstate Commerce, of which Senator Cullom is chairman, to make a tour of the country and investigate the relations of American and Canadian railways and waterways. This Committee visited the cities of New York, Boston, Detroit and Chicago, and were everywhere met by the representatives of commercial interests with strong protests against any interference with Canadian railways which should cripple or destroy their most valuable and desirable competition. The question was, however, invariably asked of every witness by the committee, "Whether he thought Canadian railways should be subjected to the same regulations and restraints as were imposed upon American railways." Of course every witness invariably answered that he did, even if at the same time he questioned the necessity of a Senate committee making a tour of the country to ask a question which could have but one answer.

This committee on "The general relations of Canada and the United States" continued the investigation of the railroad question at the cities of Minneapolis, St. Paul, Tacoma, Portland (Oregon) and San Francisco, and met with the same protests from commercial interests. The representatives of the competing railway interests, who appeared before the committees almost invariably urged some legislation which should, as they diplomatically phrased it, " impose upon the Canadian lines the same regulations and restrictions as those placed by law upon American lines." This fair seeming proposition was, as before mentioned, cordially assented to by all classes of witnesses, and it only remained to point out the particulars wherein the law discriminated in the carrying of American traffic in favor of the Canadian lines and against their American rivals. The testimony, however, *reveals no attempt by any American railway representative to specifically point out such a discrimination.*

As there was no cross-examination of witnesses, and some of the testimony consists of elaborately written statements or briefs, some extremely ill-founded and inaccurate statements of alleged facts, necessarily passed unchallenged.

The reasons alleged by their American competitors for further legislative restriction or regulation of Canadian railroads group themselves as follows:

1st. The advantages of Canadian railroads by reason of excessive governmental subsidies and foreign capital.

2d. The diversion to Canadian railroads of traffic which naturally belongs to American railroads.

(*a*) Transcontinental traffic of American origin and destination; (*b*) transpacific traffic to the Canadian Pacific railroad.

3d. The advantage of the Canadian railroads in their local traffic, the Interstate Commerce Act enabling them to recoup their losses on long-haul American traffic by high local rates.

4th. The lower cost of operation of Canadian railroads.

5th. The differentials which American railroads are compelled to grant to their Canadian competitors.

6th. The destruction of the revenues of American lines by excessive competition.

7th. The national policy of protection should apply to American railroads as well as to American merchants and manufacturers.

Six of these reasons must stand or fall according to the facts which either sustain or disprove them. The seventh reason rests upon a theory which, to be consistently advocated, must coincide with the general policy of those who proclaim it. My purpose is, therefore, to confine myself mainly to the facts which underlie this great question, in full confidence that their unprejudiced consideration will disprove each and every one of these alleged reasons.

FIRST REASON—EXCESSIVE SUBSIDIES AND FOREIGN CAPITAL.

These features of railway construction are as characteristic of American as of Canadian lines. The vast sums contributed to American railways by federal, State and municipal authorities are well known. Mr. Patterson, a member of the Union Pacific Railroad Commission, states in his report, that "governmental aid to that corporation will have amounted in 1895, when the obligations mature, to *four hundred and forty-seven millions of dollars.*"

Mr. C. P. Huntington, president of the Southern Pacific Railroad said to the House Committee on Pacific Railroads, in the Fiftieth Congress, that "the government made a land grant to the Northern Pacific Railroad of much greater value than the lands and bonds together which were granted to the Central and the Union Pacific companies."

The immensely valuable subventions to the Southern Pacific and Atlantic and Pacific companies are matters of history. Pennsylvania, Maryland, New York, Massachusetts and Illinois, and the cities of Philadelphia, Baltimore and Cincinnati are notable examples of State and municipal aid to railroads. Our friends across the border have been but feeble imitators of ourselves in these matters. It is absurd to claim that either country in thus seeking to develop its transportation interests has been influenced by a feeling of political or commercial hostility to the other.

The Grand Trunk railroad, as at present organized, has not been the recipient of any considerable government aid. One of the original companies now consolidated into the main organization did, in 1852, receive a government loan of $15,000,000, which has never been returned and on which no interest is paid. The Canadian Pacific company has received fairly liberal assistance from the Dominion Government, but small in comparison with American transcontinental lines, and very much less than the amount claimed by its American competitors.

The following table was submitted to the committee last year by one witness, who claimed it to be a reliable statement of the subventions granted to the Canadian Pacific company. Notwithstanding repeated denials from official sources, this table has been widely quoted as authoritative and true by the press, and even on the floor of the United States Senate.

In view of the fact that Mr. Van Horne, the president of the Canadian Pacific company, at a hearing of the Senate Committee on Interstate commerce held in New York in May, 1889, showed the utter untruthfulness of the table, it is difficult to understand the statement by its author to this committee in April, 1890, that "the president of the Canadian Pacific railroad has conceded that this is a correct statement of the direct aids which the company has received from the Dominion Government." The following is the table as found on page 896 of the testimony already taken by this committee:

Revised estimate of gifts from the Dominion Government to the Canadian Pacific Railway Company, and securities which that company has been enabled to float (stock and bonds) as the result of the Dominion guaranty and the land grant of 25,000,000 acres of land:

Cash subsidies as follows:
1. (a) Subsidy of $25,000,000 mentioned in section 8 of act of February 15, 1881; (b) 714 miles of railroad constructed by the Dominion Government, costing $35,000,000, which was presented to the Canadian Pacific Company as a gift, with interest to June 30, 1887). (See Public Accounts of Canada for 1887.) $61,760,785
2. Capital stock originally $100,000,000, but reduced to $55,000,000, with a dividend of 3 per cent. guaranteed for ten years. (See Poor's Manual) 65,000,000
3. During the session of Parliament of 1884 the Dominion Government authorized a loan to the company of $29,880,916, to be paid as the work of construction continued, and for the purpose of expediting construction. Of this amount $9,880,912 is secured by lien on the entire road and land grant, subject to the then outstanding land-grant bonds; also government bonds to the amount of $20,000,000, which were exchanged for a like amount of the company's loan of $35,000,000, which had been issued in the place of the $35,000,000 of original stock which had been retired. (See sec. 4, act 20, July, 1885) 29,880,912
4. Balance of $35,000 000 loan, after deducting $20,000,000, placed in the hands of the government, in order to secure the $20,000,000 bonds above mentioned 15,000,000
5. Land-grant bonds issued by the company as a lien upon the lands which it acquired by gift of the Dominion 25,000,000
6. Bonds, interest guaranteed by the Dominion for fifty years at 3½ per cent., issued to the company for the purpose of remunerating it for the loss of its relinquishment of the monopoly of railroad building in Manitoba 15,000,000
7. Subsidy of $186,000 a year for twenty years to line through the State of Maine 3,720,000

Total $215,361,697

" Of this total sum about $105,000,000 may be classed as cash and gifts available as cash, and $110,000,000 as guaranties of securities.

The president of the Canadian Pacific Railroad has conceded that this is a correct statement of direct aids which the company has received from the Dominion Government."

The joining by the northwestern British Provinces of the Canadian Federation, in 1867, was made conditional upon the building by the government of a trans-continental railroad affording direct communication between them and the middle and maritime provinces. The government accordingly undertook the construction of the Canadian Pacific Railroad. Large sums of money were wastefully spent in surveying several possible routes, and finally 714 miles were constructed in the extravagant and unbusinesslike manner characteristic of most governmental enterprises. The line consisted of three detached portions, one extending eastward from the Pacific coast, one along a portion of the north shore of Lake Superior, and one southward from Winnipeg towards the United States boundary. Thirty-five millions of dollars had thus been expended, a large proportion of which had been wasted, and the government finding itself unable to complete the enterprise short of bankruptcy, and still bound by its solemn pledge to the northwestern provinces, offered to any private company which would complete the work, to donate the 714 miles already built, $25,000,000 in cash, 25,000,000 of acres of land, exemption from taxation and certain monopoly privileges against the building of other lines for a specified term of years. President Van Horne stated under oath in New York in May, 1889, that these widely separated lines composing the 714 miles above mentioned, and which had cost the government $35,000,000 were worth practically nothing to his company. That he was obliged to abandon the government surveys which had cost several millions of dollars, and make new ones, that the cost of the remainder of the line was largely increased by reason of being obliged to connect it with the unwisely located 714 miles, and that even as they stood he could have duplicated them with $12,000,000. It is evident then that the first item of the table should stand at $37,000,000.

The capital stock was finally fixed at $65,000,000, but not a dollar of it was ever purchased or owned by the Dominion Government and is not now. Every share of it was purchased and paid for by private parties and the proceeds were applied to the discharge of the Company's obligations, or to the construction of its railroad. The assertion then that the capital stock was a gift from the government is simply an unblushing and reckless disregard for the truth.

The government guarantee of a 3 per cent dividend for

ten years was not a gift, but an annuity purchased from the government by the Company with an actual deposit of cash. The second item of this table may therefore be safely set down at nil.

The third item is so clumsily stated as not to convey a very intelligible idea of the author's meaning. It is insinuated rather than stated that the Dominion Government issued its own obligations to the amount of $20,000,000, and turned them over to the company. This is wholly untrue. The facts which are supposed to be concealed within the depths of this hazy item, are briefly these. The stock panic in 1884 involving the financial failure of Grant & Ward, Henry Villard, and others, created such distrust in monetary circles, that the Canadian Pacific Company found it difficult if not impossible to market its stock and securities, and the construction of its railroad would have ceased but for the temporary assistance furnished by the government. Parliament authorized a loan to the company, on a blanket mortgage covering all its assets, at 4 per cent which amounted finally to $35,000,000. It then authorized a reduction in the capital stock of the company from $100,000,000 to $65,000,000. It then granted to the company the power to issue in lieu of the $35,000,000 of stock thus cancelled, $35,000,000 of its own bonds bearing interest at 5 per cent. These bonds were sold to the public in London, New York and elsewhere, and from their proceeds $25,000,000 in cash were paid into the Dominion treasury towards the satisfaction of the temporary loan. This left $10,000,000 still unpaid, which was liquidated by the return to the government of enough of its land-grant at $1.50 per acre (about 7,000,000 acres) to pay the balance. The *gift* represented therefore in this item should stand at $10,000,000.

The fourth item is a bungling repetition of a part of the transactions covered by the third item, and should therefore be cut out, or stand at nil.

The fifth item is a true statement. The bonds were issued by the company and secured by the lands given to it by the government. These bonds have since that time been redeemed by the company and the lands are now pledged for other purposes, as will subsequently appear. This item should therefore stand at $25,000,000.

The sixth item states correctly the transaction involved, but has no place in a schedule of gifts. Upon the organization of the Canadian Pacific Company, the government agreed that no line of railroad leading southward from the Canadian Pacific Railroad to the United States boundary, should be built for a period of twenty years. This was to insure traffic to the division of the railroad lying north of Lake Superior, as the barren country through which it runs could furnish it little or no local traffic. The Manitoba people desired to build a railroad of their own to the international boundary, and vigorously and even violently demanded a rescission by the government of its contract with the Canadian Pacific Company. This monopoly privilege was of material value to the company in marketing its securities, and its cancellation was likely to interfere with their sale. To relieve the company from this embarrassment and at the same time placate the people of Manitoba, the government agreed that for the surrender of so much of the contract, it would guarantee $3\frac{1}{2}$ per cent. interest on $15,000,000 of the company's fifty year bonds. The government's guaranty is secured by a lien on all the unsold lands of the company, proceeds of all sales of which are to be received directly into the Dominion treasury, until such a sinking fund shall be accumulated as will reimburse the government for the interest and principal of the bonds at maturity. The lien is then to be cancelled, and the unsold lands are to revert to the control of the company. This item should clearly, therefore, be stricken from the list of "gifts."

The seventh item also rests on misstatement. Some years

ago, before the Canadian Pacific Railroad was built, the Maritime Provinces complained of the long and round about route via the Intercolonial Railroad, and demanded a shorter line to Montreal. The Dominion government thereupon offered a subsidy of $186,000 per annum for twenty years to any company which would build a short line via the State of Maine. The International Railroad Co. of Canada and Maine was formed to build the line. It failed to do so, and subsequently sold its franchise, including the subsidy, to the Atlantic & Northwestern Railroad Co. This company, unable to complete the line, transferred its franchise, and subsidy to the Canadian Pacific company under a lease. This subsidy was therefore acquired by the Canadian Pacific company by purchase, and not by gift. This item must also be stricken from the table. To recapitulate:

Corrected list of gifts received by the Canadian Pacific Railroad from the Dominion Government.

In cash $25,000,000
In partly built railroad lines............ 12,000,000
In cash for lands surrendered............... 10,000,000
In lands on which bonds have been issued for.. 25,000,000

Total direct gifts..................$72,000,000

To stretch a point, it might be assumed that without the land grant as security, the government would never have guaranteed the interest on the $15,000,000 of 50-year bonds, and adding this to the amount produced by the donated lands, and it would only show a total of $87,000,000. Even this amount as compared with the $215,361,697, given in the table of the witness referred to, shows either a sad degree of ignorance or a serious misstatement of facts.

The *bete noir* of the American railroads is the annual subsidy granted the Canada Pacific Railway by the imperial government for the carriage of the mails between Halifax and Asiatic ports (not between Vancouver and Asiatic ports, as is popularly stated), amounting to three hundred thousand dollars, one-half of which goes to the land portion and one-half to the ocean portion of the route. Up to this time none of this subsidy has been paid, and none is due until the completion of certain steamships now building under the supervision of the British admiralty, and which are to begin service some time in April, 1891. The following figures are compiled from the Second Annual Report of Railway Statistics to the Interstate Commerce Commission for the year ending June 30, 1889. For the purpose of painting the advantages of the foreign line in the strongest colors the unearned and unreceived subsidy shall be added to the postal compensation received by the Canada Pacific railway for the year ending June 30, 1889, and the total compared with that received by some of its American competitors for the same time.

Canadian Pacific Railway—Mail compensation, $306,591; subsidy, $150,000; total, $456,591.

Vanderbilt System—Composed of various roads, $3,409,482.

Pennsylvania System — Composed of various roads, $2,262,001.

Union Pacific System—$1,056,711.

Southern Pacific Railway—$979,499.

Northern Pacific Railway—$443,638.

If, therefore, postal subsidies or postal compensation, or both, measure the ability of one railroad system to compete with another, the American systems are in no danger of losing the race.

If legislation is to be directed against railroads because they are built by foreign capital, many of our American roads would be in a pitiable condition, for it is a well-known fact that some of our leading roads are largely owned abroad, and the foreign capital now invested in American railroads would build several Canadian Pacific systems. The stock and bond capital of that system is, as given on page

212 of the Annual Report, etc., above mentioned, a fraction in excess of one hundred and thirteen millions of dollars, while the annual remittance for interest and dividends on American railroads to England, Germany and Holland, is stated on reliable authority to aggregate about one hundred millions of dollars.

If foreign capital *per se* is deserving of hostile legislation, some tax or restriction should at once be imposed upon the English millions now represented in our great breweries, flouring mills, elevators, tobacco factories and other enterprises.

SECOND REASON.—DIVERSION OF TRAFFIC FROM AMERICAN RAILROADS.

The first subdivision of this reason is the diversion of traffic which has an American origin and destination, viz., between San Francisco via steamer to Vancouver (some 800 miles), thence via Canadian Pacific to American cities east of the Missouri River. The subjoined table tells its own story and destroys this scarecrow:

	Tons.	Earnings.
Total transcontinental traffic carried by *all* the Transcontinental Association lines for twelve months ending June 31, 1889	744,921	$17,146,641 24
Total "States to States" traffic carried by the Canadian Pacific Railway via Vancouver for same period	12,852½	214,811 90
Percentage carried by the Canadian Pacific	1.72	1.25

The utter insignificance of this diversion renders it almost unnecessary to make further reference to east-bound transcontinental traffic, but the peculiar methods of dealing with it displayed by Mr. A. M. Towne, general manager of the Southern Pacific Railway, in his "open letter" to this Senate Committee, deserve a passing notice. Mr. Towne makes a startling display of items of freight and the weight of each, all nicely *reduced to pounds*. To the unaccustomed eye the ravages of the Canadian competitor thus present a harrowing picture. Reduce Mr. Towne's figures to car-loads of fifteen tons each and the following is the result:

Number of car-loads via Canadian Pacific, 12 months of 1887..., ... 485
Number of car-loads via Canadian Pacific, 16 months to April 30, 1889............................ 333
Average number of cars per month, 29 ; per day, 1.
Average number of cars crossing Detroit river (Customs Report) per day, 1,000 (about).

I make the comparison of "the diversion" with the daily traffic at this city merely to give a clearer idea of its insignificance. The average on west-bound States to States traffic is slightly higher, but does not merit further attention.

The second subdivision of this reason is the diversion of transpacific traffic, which, it is claimed, naturally belongs to, and but for the Canadian Pacific Railway would be carried by the American lines. The principal items composing this traffic are tea, domestics, and silk. I subjoin a table of the tea imports from Japan for fourteen years into the United States and Canada and the routes by which they were carried. The statistics are reliable, and were obtained from Messrs. Smith, Baker & Co., one of the oldest and most influential American firms in the tea trade, having houses established in Yokohama and Kobe, Japan, and a house in New York under the supervision of Mr. R. B. Smith, the resident partner there :

Imports of Teas into United States and Canada from Japan, 1875 to 1889, Inclusive.

Season.	Via San Francisco.	Via Vancouver.	Via Suez.	Sailer to New York.	Via Tacoma.	Total.
1875–'6......	13,323,946	....	1,906,235	9,980,621	....	25,210,802
1876–'7......	11,110,057	....	5,337,980	5,982,300	....	22,430,337
1877–'8......	14,448 229	....	5 590,647	3,232,708	....	23,271.584
1878–'9......	12,209.728	....	12,028,604	1,262 248	....	25,500,580
1879–'80.....	17,222,299	....	15,092,653	2,334 527	....	34,649,479
1880–'1......	18,317,027	....	20 167.157	1,013,776	....	39,497,960
1881–'2......	19.718.806	....	14,549,262	....	....	34,268,068
1882–'3......	12.333 987	....	21,668 376	532,422	....	34,534,785
1883–'4......	16,217,369	....	18,017,876	22,538	....	34,257,783
1884–'5......	15,589,961	....	19,818,428	....	....	35,408,389
1885–'6......	19,018,022	....	16,730,911	315 951	2,998,517	39.003,401
1886–'7......	21,972,555	10 322,368	12,994 502	....	....	45,289,425
1887–'8......	17.414,689	10,063.766	8.779,827	....	6,840,971	43,099,253
1888–'9......	11,908.314	9,576,580	8,848,056	248,693	9,243,404	39,820,047
1889*.......	14,242,700	5,175,557	11,559,994	103,981	6,862,537	37,924,769

*(Up to November 23, 1889, from Yokohama.) New York, January 13, 1890.

This tea "season" extends from June 1 to May 31 in each twelve months.

An inspection of the table makes it clear that "the diversion" can neither be proved nor disproved by a comparison of the quantities carried each season by any line (Mr. Towne's method), but only by a comparison of the percentages of each season's total carried by any line, as per following table:

Table Showing Percentage of Total Imports of Tea from Japan into the United States and Canada, Carried via Various Routes at Dates Named Below.

Season.	Via San Francisco, Union Pacific and Southern Pacific.	Via Tacoma, Northern Pacific.	Total via American lines.	Via steam Suez route.	Via sail vessels.	Via Vancouver, Canadian Pacific.	Total.
1875–'6........	52¾%	....	52¾%	7½%	39¾%	....	100
1882–'3...........	35¾%	....	35¾%	62 %	2¼%	....	100
1885–'6.................... ..	48½%	7¾%	56¼%	42¾%	1 %	....	100
1886–'7...........	48½%	....	48½%	28½%	....	23 %	100
1887–'8..........................	40½%	15¾%	56¼%	20¼%	....	23½%	100
1888–'9..........................	30 %	23¼%	53¼%	22¼%	....	24½%	100
To November 23, 1889........	37½%	17¾%	55¼%	30 %	....	14¾%	100

The percentage via San Francisco and via Tacoma must be added to show the total percentage via American lines for comparison with any other route or routes for the given season.

The percentage carried by the American lines for the "season" then in progress, which ended May 31, 1890, indicates, as shown by the table, that the American lines would that "season" carry a larger share of the traffic than at any time since 1875, both in tonnage and percentage. The irresistible conclusion is that "the diversion" via the Canada Pacific route has been almost wholly at the expense of British steamers and sailing vessels, and that the disastrous effect of its competition claimed by the American lines is a pure myth.

That this statement is correct, is placed absolutely beyond controversy, by the following extracts from the testimony in a case tried before the Interstate Commerce Commission in June last. This case is known as the "Import Rate Case," in which I had the honor to appear as counsel for the Canadian Pacific Railroad Co., which was one of twenty-eight respondents. The complainants were the New York Board of Trade and Transportation, the Commercial Exchange of Philadelphia, and the San Francisco Board of Trade.

Extract from testimony on pages 193, 194, and 195:

MR. RAYMOND—So these figures are probably the net figures. But you say that three-fourths of the teas, anyway, that come to the Pacific coast are Japan teas?

MR. STUBBS (Vice-president Southern Pacific Railway Co.)—That is my estimate—that about three-fourths of the teas that pass through the Pacific coast are Japan teas. Northern Pacific teas, I believe, are all Japan teas.

MR. RAYMOND—Do you know, Mr. Stubbs, whether the percentages of the totals received on the Pacific coast carried by San Francisco and Tacoma together have, relative to the total receipts on the coast, increased or decreased during the last three years?

MR. STUBBS—I think they have increased, sir.

Mr. Raymond—*The American lines, then, have increased their tonnage?*

Mr. Stubbs—*I think so; yes, sir.*

Mr. Raymond—Do you know anything about what the percentage of increase has been?

Mr. Stubbs—No, sir; I have not figured it. The increase is slight. The reason for it is that we have been forced to make low rates, *and the tea has been diverted from Suez to these lines.*

Mr. Raymond—What has been the course of the percentage of the total brought via Vancouver during the last three years?

Mr. Stubbs—I do not know. I have not gone into that.

Mr. Raymond—Then on what do you base your statement that the competition of the Canadian Pacific is taking your traffic away?

Mr. Stubbs—I gave you the figures as to 1889-'90—one year.

Mr. Raymond—But I am asking you about *percentages* for three or four years previous.

Mr. Stubbs—I say I do not know, because I have not figured it out. I did not charge my mind with that.

Mr. Raymond—If it is true, Mr. Stubbs, that the percentages of the total imports of tea on the coast during the last three years have *increased* via San Francisco and Tacoma, and have *decreased* at Vancouver, then it is not true, is it, that the Canadian Pacific is diverting your traffic by cutting rates all to pieces, or that sort of thing?

Mr. Stubbs—What might be true—

Mr. Raymond—Can't you answer that question?

Mr. Martin, counsel for the Southern Pacific R. R. Co.—Let him answer in his own way.

Mr. Stubbs—What might be true as to last year need not be true as to this year, and what I say as to the Canadian Pacific's doings to-day is true—exactly true. They are doing just exactly what I say.

Testimony on page 231:

Mr. PETTIT, counsel of Philadelphia Exchange—In the east-bound business from San Francisco, as I understand you, you got a better rate when you had only the vessel competition to meet.

Mr. STUBBS—Because we were content with a less proportion of the total traffic.

Mr. PETTIT—As soon as you wanted a greater proportion of the traffic, then you had to reduce the rate?

Mr. STUBBS—More lines came on, and that necessitated it. We could not keep our proportion. The Canadian Pacific came on, and it must have some traffic. Necessarily that traffic must either come from us or from the other competitors. It made the rates to get it. That forced the rates down by all the lines, and they forced them low enough to get a good proportion. *We have retained our proportion at lower rates, and they took what they got, you may say, from the other competitors.*

Testimony on page 167:

Mr. MARTIN—This Suez route has heretofore dictated the rate?

Mr. STUBBS—*Always! Yes, sir;* with the exception of the small quantity that we were enabled to get of the early teas, on which we arbitrarily charged, regardless of any competition, 5 cents a pound before the Canadian Pacific came in. We were able to get that on one or two cargoes, but after the desire for quick transportation ceased we had to follow them right down to get any share of it.

The testimony of Mr. Heiman, a tea merchant with houses in Yokohama and Hiogo, Japan, is conclusive as to the influence of the Suez route upon traffic.

Page 125:

Mr. MARTIN—How do these rates ordinarily compare with each other, the Suez by steamer, and rail across the continent, and Suez by sailing vessels?

Mr. Heiman—The Suez route is generally slightly the cheapest. The cause of that is the sail and rail via Tacoma to the United States and steamer and rail via San Francisco and Vancouver.

Page 128:

Mr. Martin—What would be the effect upon the traffic across the continent by steamer to the Pacific coast and by rail from the Pacific coast, if we should make any material increase in rates?

Mr. Heiman—We would not ship that way at all.

Mr. Martin—Would the traffic be lost to the American ships?

Mr. Heiman—*We would give it to Suez.* Sometimes it does come that way. Last year the steamships kept rates up, and they lost a great deal of cargo in consequence. It came by Suez.

Page 129:

Mr. Martin—This rate on tea to the Pacific coast is controlled by the rate made by the Suez steamers?

Mr. Heiman—*Yes, sir; certainly.*

Mr. Martin—They can carry it cheaper than the others, can they not?

Mr. Heiman—Except for the first boat of the season, then the steamers get a much higher rate. This year they had one cargo at 3½ cents a pound, *but directly the crop comes forward in quantity the Suez rate rules the market.*

Page 131:

Commissioner Veazy—How does it happen that it costs you $1.50 by San Francisco when you could get it at 70 cents via Suez?

Mr. Heiman—There is a saving in time and insurance, and probably they may not keep their rate at 1½ cents; it may go down in the next week.

Mr. Martin—This question of rate becomes a question of carriage. *When they cannot meet this competition by Suez the railroads then get the trade?*

Mr. HEIMAN—Yes, sir.

The statistics before referred to, also justify the statement, that the total tea tonnage of the Canadian Pacific route *does not equal the local consumption of Canada herself.* The annual average imports of tea from China and Japan into Canada for the last five years equals about 19,000,000 pounds, of this amount 37.40/100 per cent comes through American seaports and over American railroads.

American railroads claim serious damage from the diversion to the Canadian Pacific route of the transportation of domestics or cotton goods to China and Japan.

The fact is that the American transcontinental lines have *never* carried any considerable tonnage of domestics or cotton goods for any trans-pacific destination. I would be glad to have the American lines produce any figures which will disprove my assertion. Before the Canadian Pacific route was opened, the small export trade in American cottons was done by rail from the mills to Fall River, Mass., thence by water to New York, and thence to China and Japan by British vessels, via the Suez canal. A suggestive and instructive prophecy, which is being rapidly fulfilled, was made by Hon. George F. Page, of Concord, N. H., in his argument on behalf of the business interests of New Hampshire before the railroad committee of the New Hampshire Legislature, July 28, 1887, in favor of the passage of House Bill No. 28. Mr. Page says:

"On behalf of a large number of business men, and especially the manufacturers in Merrimac Valley, I desire to submit a few suggestions for your consideration. I am not here in the interest of any railroad corporation or of the agent of any railroad corporation. What I say to-night will be said as my own voluntary action.

* * * "Before the civil war, New England had a large trade in cotton cloth with China. The war destroyed that trade, as it did nearly all our export business. England, with her commercial enterprise, seized the trade, and has practically monopolized it since. Prior to the war, there was an open competition in the Chinese markets between old England and New England, cotton cloth being shipped by both peoples around the Cape of Good Hope; but it was necessary to put it into tin cases or otherwise sealed packages to protect the cloth from atmospheric changes, for without this precaution through the long voyage through the southern seas it would mildew, and therefore would not arrive in a merchantable condition. You will remember that before we could recover our export trade after the war, England secured control of the Suez Canal, and she has ever since held this cotton trade with China almost exclusively by virtue of that fact, for in shipping through the Suez Canal by steamer, the English manufacturers are not obliged to pack their goods in tin cases, but they put a kind of varnish or dressing as a coating over their packages, which, while it does not entirely exclude the air, does it to a sufficient extent to protect the goods on a short voyage through a moist climate. These conditions have put an embargo upon the shipment of cotton cloth in any considerable amount from the United States to those markets, while the amount of cloth shipped by English manufacturers to China yearly has already reached 400,000,000 yards and to Java 100,000,000 yards. *That trade belongs to New England, and may be recovered, at least in part, if not entirely, by New England.*

"With the completion of the Canadian Pacific Railway and the putting on of a regular line of steamers from Vancouver to Shanghai and Hong Kong, the way is open to this consummation, provided we can make proper connections with that road. By this route, cotton goods can be shipped from New England even without the expense of the dressing which the English manufacturers apply to their packages shipped through the Suez Canal. Instead of that, we can ship the cloth in ordinary bales or boxes, because, the voyage being a short one and wholly in a northern latitude, the condition of the goods upon arrival will be the same as when they left the factory.

"The time required for the shipping of the goods from the New England mills to Shanghai is about thirty days; the time from England, via the Suez Canal, is about fifty-three days. Some one may say that England may ship her cloth across the Atlantic and thence over the Canadian route to Shanghai; but suppose she does. The raw cotton must be taken across the Atlantic and the finished goods returned, and both the expense and time are against the English manufacturer. So it is that, while New England has not been able in the past successfully to compete with old England, with this proposed transportation system completed, old England cannot successfully compete with New England.

"This, gentlemen, is no picture of the imagination, for while we discuss this question here, a train of twenty cars is on its way with fifteen hundred bales of cotton cloth for Japan and China. That train passed up through the Merrimac Valley, thence over the Canadian Pacific Railway to Vancouver, from which points these goods will be taken by steamer to Yokohama and Shanghai. To-night a vast commerce has its birth, for China, as if impatient of delay and unwilling to await the slow process of legislation, but anticipating what that legislation is to be, reaches out her hand and bids New England 'welcome.'"

A year ago while I was in the office of the Canadian Pacific Steamship Company, in New York, an agent of one of the New England mills called for the purpose of obtaining a rate on 1,000 cases of twills to Bombay. This simple fact speaks volumes, indicating as it does that by means of this foreign railway corporation, America may yet market her domestic manufactures among the teeming millions of Britain's own India. In view of these facts, how can your honorable committee heed the complaints of American trans-continental lines which have never been willing to make any rates by which New England could be aided in securing this business?

As to the item of raw silk. It is true that the Canadian Pacific Railway, by means of special silk express trains and great energy, has diverted from American lines a portion of the traffic which was wholly their own. The extent of the diversion is shown by the following table:

Imports of Raw Silk, May 1, 1888, to March 27, 1889.
American lines.

Via Pacific Mail Steamship Company	8,521 bales.
" Occidental and Oriental Steamship Company	7,854 "
" Canadian Pacific Steamship Company	3,353 "
Total	19,728 bales.

Proportion of Canadian Pacific, 17 per cent.

Third Reason—Local Tariffs.

In order to intelligently consider this reason I have caused to be compiled from the books of the Grand Trunk Railway Company and from the books of the Canadian Pacific Railway Company the local tariffs in force in 1889 on certain staple articles of freight for distances from five miles to four hundred miles inclusive. The comparison is made with the rates in force at the same time upon twenty American railroads for the same articles of freight for the same distances.

The articles of freight are as follows:

Flour and wheat
Iron
Sugar.

Boots and shoes.
Agricultural implements.
Salt.
Lumber.
Hardware (N. O. S.*)

It will be noted that on the article of salt the comparison is made with seventeen, but on all other articles with twenty railroads. The names of the American railroads are:

Northern Pacific.
Southern Pacific.
Pennsylvania.
Illinois Central.
Chicago, Milwaukee & St Paul.
Boston & Lowell.
Chicago & Northwestern.
Chicago, St. Paul, Minneapolis & Omaha.
Chicago & Alton.
Chicago, St. Paul & Kansas City.
Chicago, Kansas & Nebraska.
Chicago, Burlington & Quincy.
Deleware, Lackawanna & Western.
Hannibal & St. Joe.
Minneapolis, St Paul & Sault St. Marie.
New York & New England.
Passumpsic.
Toledo, Ann Arbor & North Michigan.
Wabash.
Cincinnati, Jackson & Mackinaw.

I subjoin a table showing the comparison *in extenso* of the Canadian lines with the first four American lines mentioned, selecting the two highest and two lowest. The tariffs of the remaining sixteen lines I have filed with the Com-

(*Not otherwise specified.)

mittee on Interstate Commerce for the verification of my analysis and conclusion. The Canadian lines show two local tariffs, mileage and special, the former being used in small station to station business where volume of traffic is small and non-competitive, the special being applicable to all stations of any considerable size or importance.

A careful comparison of the Grand Trunk tariffs with those of the Canadian Pacific shows very little difference, the latter being slightly the lowest, so that the conclusions favorable to the Grand Trunk are even more so to its Canadian rival.

Flour and Wheat—In Car-Loads in Cents per 100 Lbs.

Miles.	G. T. R.		C. P. R.		N. Pac.	S. Pac	Pa.R.R.	Ill. Cen.
	Mileage.	Special.	Mileage.	Special.	Local.	Local.	Local.	Local.
5	3	4	3	4	3	4	5	4½
10	4	4	4	4	4	6	6	4¾
15	5	4	5	4	4½	10	6	5
20	6	4	6	4	5	14	7	5
25	7	5	7	5	5½	17	7	5¼
30	8	5	8	5	0	21	8	5½
35	8	6	8	5	6½	24	8	5¾
40	9	6	9	6	7	29	9	6
45	9	6	9	6	7½	32	9	6
50	10	6	10	6	8	36	9	6¼
75	12	7	12	7	10	54	11	7¼
100	14	7	14	7	12	72	13	8
125	15	7	15	8	13	90	15	8¾
150	16	10	16	10	14½	109	16	9½
175	18	10	18	10	15½	110	17	10¼
200	19	11	19	13	17	110	18	10¾
250	20	13	20	15	19½	110	19	12¼
300	23	14½	23	15	22	110	21	13¼
350	24	16½	24	16½	24	110	23	14¾
400	25	17½	25	17½	26	110	24	16¼

IRON—In Car-Loads in Cents per 100 Lbs.

Miles.	G. T. R.		C. P. R.		N. Pac.	S. Pac.	Pa.R.R.	Ill. Cen.
	Mileage.	Special.	Mileage.	Special.	Local.	Local.	Local.	Local.
5	4	....	4	....	5	4	4	5
10	5	....	5	....	7	6	5	5¼
15	6	....	6	6	9	10	6	5½
20	7	....	7	6	10	14	6	5¾
25	8	....	8	7	11	17	7	6
30	9	....	9	8	13	21	7	6
35	10	....	10	8	14	24	7	6¼
40	11	....	11	8	15	29	7	6½
45	12	....	12	8	16	32	7½	6¾
50	12	....	12	8	17	36	7½	7
75	15	....	15	8	22	54	10	7¾
100	18	15	18	8	27	72	12	8½
125	19	18	19	8	30	90	13	9¾
150	20	18	20	9	32	109	14	11¼
175	22	19	22	9	35	110	15	12¾
200	23	20	23	11	37	110	16½	14¼
250	26	23	26	11	42	110	18	17
300	30	25	30	11	47	110	20	20
350	33	27	33	15	52	110	21	22½
400	35	30	35	15	57	110	22½	25

SUGAR—In Car-Loads in Cents per 100 Lbs.

Miles.	G. T. R.		C. P. R.		N. Pac.	S. Pac.	Pa.R.R	Ill. Cen.
	Mileage.	Special.	Mileage.	Special.	Local.	Local.	Local.	Local.
5	4	....	4	....	5	4	5	4
10	5	....	5	....	7	6	6	5¼
15	6	6	6	6	9	10	6	5½
20	7	6	7	6	10	14	7	5¾
25	8	7	8	7	11	17	7	6
30	9	8	9	8	13	21	8	6¼
35	10	8	10	8	14	24	8	6½
40	11	8	11	8	15	29	9	6½
45	12	8	12	8	16	32	9	6¾
50	12	8	12	8	17	36	9	7
75	15	8	15	8	22	54	11	7
100	18	8	18	8	27	72	13	8
125	19	8	19	8	29	90	15	9¾
150	20	9	20	9	32	110	16	11
175	22	9	22	9	34	110	17	12¾
200	23	11	23	11	37	110	18	14
250	26	11	26	11	42	110	19	17
300	30	11	30	11	47	110	21	20
350	33	12	33	15	52	110	23	22
400	35	15	35	15	57	110	24	25

BOOTS AND SHOES—In Less than Car-Loads in Cents per 100 Lbs.

Miles.	G. T. R.		C. P. R.		N. Pac.	S. Pac.	Pa.R.R.	Ill. Cen.
	Mileage.	Special.	Mileage.	Special.	Local.	Local.	Local.	Local.
5	8	....	8	....	10	4	6	14
10	10	....	10	....	14	7	6	14
15	12	12	12	12	17	11	9	15
20	14	12	14	12	20	15	10	16
25	16	14	16	14	22	18	13	17
30	18	15	18	15	25	22	14	17
35	20	16	20	16	27	25	14	18
40	22	16	22	16	30	30	16	18
45	24	16	24	16	32	35	18	19
50	24	16	24	16	34	37	20	20
75	30	20	30	20	44	55	26	22
100	36	21	36	22	54	75	29	24
125	38	22	38	22	60	93	32	28
150	40	22	40	22	64	112	34	32
175	44	22	44	22	70	130	38	36
200	46	24	46	24	74	150	42	40
250	52	28	52	28	84	168	48	48
300	60	28	60	28	94	187	54	56
350	66	30	66	30	104	200	58	58
400	70	40	70	34	114	200	61	61

AGRICULTURAL IMPLEMENTS—In Car-Loads in Cents per 100 Lbs.

Miles.	G. T. R.		C. P. R.		N. Pac.	S. Pac.	Pa.R.R.	Ill. Cen.
	Mileage.	Special.	Mileage.	Special.	Local.	Local.	Local.	Local.
5	4	....	4	....	4	4	4	5
10	5	....	5	....	6	6	5	5¼
15	6	....	6	....	7	10	6	5½
20	6	....	6	....	8	14	6	5¾
25	7	6	7	6	9	17	7	6
30	8	7	8	6	10	21	7	6¼
35	9	7	9	7	11	24	7	6½
40	10	7	10	7	12	29	7	6¾
45	11	7	11	7	13	32	7½	6¾
50	11	7	11	7	14	36	7½	7
75	14	9	14	9	18	54	10	8
100	16	10	16	10	23	72	12	9
125	17	10	17	12	24	90	13	10¾
150	18	10	18	13	26	109	14	12¼
175	20	10	20	13	27	110	15	14¼
200	21	11	21	13	30	110	16½	16¼
250	24	13	24	13	34	110	18	19½
300	30	13	30	13	38	110	20	22½
350	31	14	31	14	42	110	21	25
400	33	18	33	18	46	110	22½	27½

Salt—In Car-Loads in Cents per 100 Lbs.

Miles.	G. T. R. Mileage.	G. T. R. Special.	C. P. R. Mileage.	C. P. R. Special.	N. Pac. Local.	S. Pac. Local.	Pa.R.R. Local.	Ill. Cen. Local.
5	3	....	3	....	3	3½	4	3¼
10	4	....	4	....	4	5	5	3½
15	4	....	4	....	4	6	5	3½
20	5	....	5	....	4	7½	6	3¾
25	5	....	5	....	5	8½	6	3¾
30	6	....	6	5	5	9½	6	4
35	6	....	6	5	6	10	6	4
40	7	....	7	6	6	11	6	4¼
45	7	....	7	6½	7	11½	7	4½
50	7	....	7	6½	8	12½	7	4½
75	10	8	10	7	11	18½	9	5
100	11	9	11	8½	13	25	10½	5¾
125	13	10	13	9	15	30	11	6¼
150	14	10	14	10	16	35	12	6¾
175	15	10	15	10	18	40	13	7¼
200	16	11	16	11	19	45	14½	7¾
250	18	12	18	12	21	50	15½	8¾
300	20	13	20	12½	23	55	16½	9¾
350	22	14	22	14	22	60	17	10¾
400	24	15	24	15	27	65	18½	11¾

Lumber—In Car-Loads in Cents per 100 Lbs.

Miles.	G. T. R. Mileage.	G. T. R. Special.	C. P. R. Mileage.	C. P. R. Special.	N. Pac. Local.	S. Pac. Local.	Pa.R.R. Local.	Ill. Cen. Local.
5	3	3	3	3	3	3	4	3½
10	4	3½	4	3½	3½	4	5	3½
15	4	4	4	4	4	5	5	3¾
20	5	4	5	4	4½	6½	6	4
25	5	5	5	5	5	7½	6	4¼
30	6	5	6	5	5½	8	6	4¼
35	6	5½	6	5½	6	8½	6	4½
40	7	5½	7	5½	6	9	6	4½
45	7	6	7	6	6½	9½	7	4¾
50	7	6	7	6	7	9½	7	5
75	10	8	10	8	9½	11	9	5½
100	11	9	11	9	11½	15	10½	6¼
125	13	9½	13	9½	13	18½	11	6¾
150	14	10	14	10	14	22½	12	7½
175	15	10	15	10	15½	26	13	8
200	16	11	16	11	16½	30	14½	8½
250	18	12½	18	12½	19	35	15½	9½
300	20	14	20	14	21½	40	16½	10½
350	22	15½	22	15½	24	45	17	11½
400	24	17	24	17	26½	50	18½	12½

HARDWARE (N. O. S.)—Less than Car-Loads in Cents per 100 Lbs.

Miles.	G. T. R.		C. P. R.		N. Pac.	S. Pac.	Pa.R.R.	Ill. Cen.
	Mileage.	Special.	Mileage.	Special.	Local.	Local.	Local.	Local.
5	7	....	7	....	9	4	6	12
10	8	....	8	....	12	7	8	12½
15	11	11	11	11	14	11	9	13¼
20	12	11	12	11	17	15	9	14
25	14	12	14	12	19	18	10	14½
30	16	13	16	13	21	22	11	15
35	18	14	18	14	23	25	12	15½
40	19	14	19	14	26	30	13	16
45	21	14	21	14	27	33	14	16½
50	21	14	21	14	29	37	16	17
75	26	18	26	18	37	55	20	18¾
100	32	18	32	18	46	75	23	20½
125	33	19	33	23	51	93	26	22¾
150	35	19	35	25	54	112	29	25¼
175	39	19	39	25	60	130	32	27¾
200	40	21	40	25	63	150	36	30¼
250	46	25	46	25	71	168	41	35
300	53	25	53	25	80	170	46	40
350	58	26	58	26	86	170	50	42½
400	61	35	61	35	97	170	53	45

I have compared each of the Grand Trunk local tariffs with the tariff of each American railroad, making 314 comparisons, in 133 of which the *average* of both the Canadian mileage and special tariffs are *higher* and in *181* comparisons *lower* than their American competitors, as per the following table:

Analysis of Comparisons of Grand Trunk Local Tariffs, Mileage and Special, with Those of Twenty American Railroads (Except on the Item of Salt, when the Comparison is with Seventeen).

Flour and wheat.	G. T. mileage higher than	15,	lower than	5,	total of	....	20
	" special "	6,	"	14,	"	....	20
Iron......	" mileage "	13,	"	7,	"	....	20
	" special "	12,	"	8,	"	....	20
Sugar....	" mileage "	14,	"	6,	"	....	20
	" special "	4,	"	16,	"	....	20
Boots and shoes.	" mileage "	10,	"	10,	"	....	20
	" special "	1,	"	19,	"	....	20
Agricultural implements	" mileage "	9,	"	11,	"	....	20
	" special "	1,	"	19,	"	....	20
Salt......	" mileage "	10,	"	7,	"	....	17
	" special "	6,	"	11,	"	....	17
Lumber..	" mileage "	13,	"	7,	"	....	20
	" special "	9,	"	11,	"	....	20
Hardware	" mileage "	10,	"	10,	"	....	20
	" special "	0,	"	20,	"	....	20
Average.........	"	133	"	181	"		314

Or, in other words, the average of both mileage and special Grand Trunk tariffs is 13¼ *per cent less* than American local tariffs.

A fairer comparison would be between the Grand Trunk special and American local tariffs, in which the result would be as follows: Grand Trunk higher than 39, lower than 118, total of 157; or in other words, the Grand Trunk special tariff is 34 *per cent less* than American local tariffs.

The relative cheapness of Grand Trunk local rates is not the result of a new policy, but has prevailed for many years, as proven by the following table, which shows a comparison in 1875 of the local rates of the then five great trunk lines of railway. The data for this table were furnished by J. L. Ringwalt, Esq., editor of "The Railway World," published at Philadelphia, Pa., and are found on page 254 of his book, entitled "Development of Transportation Systems in the United States:"

Miles from given point to station nearest the distance taken.	Kind of Freight.			
	1st Class.	2d Class.	3d Class.	4th Class.
For 50 miles:				
Erie........................... 50..	22	17	12	9
New York Central............ 55..	24	21	16	9
Pennsylvania................. 50..	19	16	14	11
Grand Trunk................. 55..	28	23	19	14
Baltimore & Ohio............ 50..	20	20	19	16
For 75 miles:				
Erie........................... 75..	27	21	15	11
New York Central............ 74..	26	23	19	13
Pennsylvania................. 75..	25	21	18	15
Grand Trunk................. 75..	30	25	20	15
Baltimore & Ohio............ 75..	30	30	25	23
For 100 miles:				
Erie........................... 100..	34	26	19	14
New York Central............ 101..	33	28	25	15
Pennsylvania................. 100..	30	25	20	15
Grand Trunk................. 103..	36	30	24	18
Baltimore & Ohio............ 100..	40	40	34	30
For 150 miles:				
Erie........................... 153..	45	34	24	19
New York Central............ 156..	48	42	36	22
Pennsylvania................. 150..	44	37	33	26
Grand Trunk................. 150..	44	37	29	22
Baltimore & Ohio............ 152..	61	50	42	36
For 200 miles:				
Erie........................... 200..	56	42	30	23
New York Central............ 199..	61	50	40	24
Pennsylvania................. 200..	66	56	46	36
Grand Trunk................. 203..	54	45	36	27
Baltimore & Ohio............ 201..	72	59	52	40
For 250 miles:				
Erie........................... 248..	67	50	36	28
New York Central............ 253..	65	53	49	28
Pennsylvania................. 250..	71	56	46	36
Grand Trunk................. 250..	60	50	40	30
Baltimore & Ohio............ 253..	95	73	60	40
For 300 miles:				
Erie........................... 300..	78	59	43	33
New York Central............ 303..	70	55	51	31
Pennsylvania................. 300..	71	56	46	36
Grand Trunk................. 300..	60	50	40	30
Baltimore & Ohio............ 300..	95	80	60	40
For 350 miles:				
Erie........................... 351..	86	65	47	38
New York Central............ 349..	76	60	50	31
Pennsylvania................. 350..	71	56	46	36
Grand Trunk................. 350..	70	58	47	35
Baltimore & Ohio............ 350..	95	80	60	40

The following analysis of the above table is based on fourth-class freight alone as a saving of time and space. A comparison of the other three classes of freight would give equally or even more favorable results. It will be noted that the name of the Baltimore & Ohio Railroad, like that of Abou Ben Adem, " leads all the rest " in high rates in 1875, as that of the Southern Pacific Railroad does in 1890:

Comparisons of Local Rates on Fourth-Class Freight of the Grand Trunk Railway Company in 1875 with those of Four American Trunk Lines.

Distances.	Grand Trunk higher than	1, same or lower than	3, or total of	4
50 miles.	" "	2, " "	2, " "	4
75 "	" "	" "	" "	4
100 "	" "	3, " "	1, " "	4
150 "	" "	1, " "	3, " "	4
200 "	" "	2, " "	2, " "	4
250 "	" "	2, " "	2, " "	4
300 "	" "	0, " "	4, " "	4
350 "	" "	1, " "	3, " "	4
Grand result............		12, " "	20, " "	32

Or in other words the Grand Trunk local tariff in 1875 was *twenty per .cent. less* than its trunk line competitors.

I have filed with the Senate Committee on Inter-State Commerce local freight tariff No. 99 of the Canadian Pacific Railway, put into effect February 1, 1888, and covering all local traffic between Winnipeg and Vancouver. This ter-titory is absolutely free from all competition by either rail or water, and the traffic is wholly dependent upon the Canadian Pacific Railway; yet for that long distance of 1,483 miles the rates are as carefully adjusted to the long-and-short-haul clause of our interstate law as by any American road. I select a few examples from this tariff:

Classes of Freight.

	1	2	3	4	5	6	7	8	9	10
Winnipeg to Aikins, 505 miles.......	151	127	102	77	70	57	39	39	57	33
Winnipeg to Golden, 1,007 miles.....	245	204	164	124	114	97	68	58	95½	56
Winnipeg to Vancouver, 1,483 miles	337	281	225	169	156	140	102	83	136	83

The schedule shows 111 stations between Winnipeg and Aikins, but not one of them pays a higher rate than as shown above. There are 168 stations between Winnipeg and Golden, 219 stations between Winnipeg and Vancouver, but no intermediate station pays more than the long-haul rate. Many of these stations are, of course, only flag stations, but the principle of the long-and-short-haul clause of our law is rigidly applied, *while on the American transcontinental lines this principle is not applied.* I select a single example from the transcontinental tariff:

Coal oil from Pittsburgh or Buffalo to
Pacific coast terminals only.............$1.25 per 100 lbs.
Coal oil from Pittsburgh or Buffalo to intermediate points east of 97th meridian ....$1.95 " " "

These rates can be found on pages 37 and 10, respectively, of the west bound transcontinental tariff now in force. This tariff also discloses that substantially the lowest rate on any American traffic from Minneapolis to Pacific coast is 99 cents per 100 lbs., while the lowest class rate for similar Canadian traffic for practically the same distance, as per Tariff No. 99, is only 83 cents per 100 lbs.

As confirmatory of the relatively lower gross earnings of the Canadian railways, I submit the following table, compiled from the Second Annual Report on the Statistics of Railways in the United States to the Interstate Commerce Commission for the year ending June 30, 1889, from page 274 to 306.

Total Traffic Earnings per Train Mile in Dollars and Fractions of a Dollar.

Canadian Pacific	$1.292
New York Central & Hudson River Railroad	1.593
Northern Pacific	1.760
Pennsylvania Railroad	1.797
Southern Pacific	1.813
Union Pacific	2.050
Chicago & Grand Trunk	1.158
Michigan Central	1.352
Lake Shore & Michigan Southern	1.632

FOURTH REASON.—LOWER COST OF OPERATION OF CANADIAN RAILROADS.

The following table compiled from the Second Annual Report on the Statistics of Railways in the United States, etc., referred to above, pages 354 to 384, proves this "reason" to be without foundation.

Percentage of Operating Expenses to Operating Income.

Canadian Pacific	65.52	per cent.
New York Central & Hudson River Railroad	64.50	"
Pennsylvania Railroad	68.11	"
Northern Pacific	60.37	"
Southern Pacific	67.44	"
Union Pacific	56.51	"
Chicago & Grand Trunk	72.27	"
Michigan Central	70.54	"
Lake Shore & Michigan Southern	63.02	"

Also the following table, compiled from the same source, pages 398 to 448:

Cost to the Following Railways of Carrying One Passenger One Mile and of Moving One Ton of Freight One Mile.

Canadian Pacific	Passenger,	1.49 cents;	freight,	.639 cents.
New York Central & Hudson River Railroad	"	1.28 "	"	.549 "
Pennsylvania Railroad	"	1.56 "	"	.486 "
Northern Pacific	"	1.61 "	"	.910 "
Southern Pacific (Pacific system)	"	1.64 "	"	.829 "
Union Pacific	"	1.83 "	"	.618 "
Chicago & Grand Trunk	"	1.41 "	"	.41 "
Michigan Central	"	1.92 "	"	.49 "
Lake Shore & Michigan Southern	"	1.70 "	"	.43 "

The net earnings of the Canadian Pacific may, however, be relatively greater than its leading competitors, owing to its lower capitalization and fixed charges, as shown by the following tables. Both its American and Canadian patrons are surely entitled to the benefit of its honest and economical construction. These tables are compiled from the same annual report of railway statistics previously cited, pages 212 to 265 and pages 398 to 448:

Amount of railway capital per mile of line operated at the close of the year ending June 30, 1889.

Canadian Pacific	36,002 dollars
Northern Pacific	81,986 "
Southern Pacific	48,550 "
Union Pacific	109,478 "

Percentage of total expenditures covered by fixed charges of the Transcontinental lines.

Canadian Pacific	28.90 per cent
Northern Pacific	39.14 "
Union Pacific	35.86 "
Southern Pacific	34.91 "

Food for thought concerning the capitalization of American transcontinental lines is found in the following remarks of Mr. C. P. Huntington before the house committee on Pacific railroads, before referred to:

"I don't like to talk about it; but, if obliged to, the Central Pacific could build a line connecting with the Union Pacific and *replace the subsidized section at one-quarter the cost of that section, and without Government aid.*"

Fifth Reason—Differential Rates Granted Canadian Railroads.

This reason has absolutely no force, from the fact that differential rates are now and always have been freely granted to numerous American railroads by the standard lines, like the Vanderbilt and Pennsylvania systems. It is merely a device for equalizing the disadvantages of greater length of line between same points, poorer equipment, less convenient terminal facilities, lack of dining car or restaurant privileges, etc.

If all hotels had strictly first-class appointments, prices would be uniform; but, as many of them are of a lower class, they attract patronage by lower prices.

Railroads follow precisely the same course, whether they are American or Canadian, with the exception that the lower prices are fixed by the consent and agreement of the first-class lines.

Present standard rates from New York to Chicago.	1st	2d	Class. 3d	4th	5th	6th
Freight traffic	75	65	50	35	30	25c. per 100 lbs.
Differentials allowed the National Dispatch	10	8	6	4	4	3	"
Kanawha Line	15	12	9	6	5	4	"
New York, Ontario & Western	8	6	4	3	2½	2	"
The West Shore, Erie, Delaware, Lackawanna & Western, and Lehigh Valley	5	4	3	2	1	1	"

Present standard rates from Chicago to New York.	1st class.	2d class.
Passenger traffic	20 dollars.	17 dollars per ticket.
Differential allowed Wabash, Chicago & Grand Trunk, Chicago & Atlantic, Nickel-Plate, and Baltimore & Ohio.	2 dollars.	1 dollar per ticket.

The above differential is allowed only when route is made in connection with the Erie, West Shore, Lackawanna, Ontario & Western, and Lehigh Valley. All of these are *American* railroads.

Between Boston and Chicago, the Boston & Albany railroad rates are the standard ones, and differentials are allowed other lines both on freight and passenger traffic. The following item in the New York *Herald* of February 2, 1890, explains itself:

"The dispute over through rates between the Boston & Albany and Fitchburg roads has been settled by arbitration. The Fitchburgh road has been awarded a differential of two dollars on each first-class passenger by the West Shore route, and three dollars by the Erie route."

The distance from Vancouver to San Francisco is 800 miles, and the only means of communication for the Canadian Pacific Railway is *one steamer per week*.

This is a disadvantage in point of time of four or five days, which, by consent and agreement of all the transcontinental lines, is equalized to the Canadian Pacific route as follows, as per transcontinental tariff, October 1, 1889:

"The rates *to San Francisco only* from points named

below via the Canadian Pacific railway will be the following differentials in cents per 100 lbs. less than the through rates shown above:"

From—	Classes of Freight.									
	1	2	3	4	5	A	B	C	D	E
St. Paul and Minneapolis	15	12	10	10	10	8	8	7	5	5
Chicago, Milwaukee, and common points	17½	14½	12	10	10	8	8	7	5	5
Cincinnati, Detroit, and common points	21	17	14	11	11	9	9	7	5	5
Pittsburgh, Buffalo, and common points	22	18	15	12	12	10½	10½	8	7	5
New York, Boston, Philadelphia, Baltimore, and common points	23	21	17	14	14	12	12	8	8	5

The differential on passenger traffic is, I think, five dollars per ticket.

It will be noted that the differentials above given apply to San Francisco only, the rates to all other Pacific coast points being precisely the same via Canadian Pacific as via other routes.

The Canadian Pacific Railway did not make a rate on American business south of the international boundary until after it was discovered that contracts were being made and rates quoted for British Columbia traffic via Puget's Sound by its American rivals. This naturally and instantly provoked retaliation and forced the Canadian Pacific to attack its competitors by seeking American traffic at Puget's Sound and San Francisco. The original purpose and policy of the Canadian Pacific is clearly shown by the following letter:

CANADIAN PACIFIC RAILWAY COMPANY,
MONTREAL, 8*th December*, 1885.

T. F. OAKES, ESQ., *Vice-President Northern Pacific Railroad, St. Paul, Minn.:*

"DEAR SIR—Our line will be open for through traffic between Eastern points and the Pacific coast in May next.

"We wish as soon as possible to consider the question of through freight and passenger tariffs. We desire to make the least possible disturbance in existing through rates and to co-operate with the existing lines in the preservation of paying tariffs. To this end I will bə glad if you will have sent us the fullest possible information as to your present rates, both regular and special, including rates on fish, fruit, etc., carried on express trains or under special conditions as to time, etc. So far as possible, we wish to adopt your existing rates, and should there be any cases in which circumstances will prevent our doing this we will communicate with you on the subject before taking any action.

      Yours truly,
"(Signed)   W. C. VAN HORN,
Vice-President.

SIXTH REASON— DESTRUCTION OF REVENUES OF AMERICAN LINES.

If the Canadian railways are diverting a large volume of traffic from their American rivals under the operation of the Interstate Commerce Act as is persistently claimed, the truth of the statement can certainly be proven by the course of their respective earnings since April, 1887, when that act took effect. I subjoin a table taken from the New York Financial Review for 1891, showing the gross earnings for the last four years inclusive, of the more prominent competitive American lines:

Northern Pacific Co.	Southern Pacific Co.
Gross Earnings for 1887....$13,854,320	Gross Earnings for 1887....$38,773,146
" " " 1888 ... 18,000,104	" " " 1888 ... 46,699,614
" " " 1889 ... 21,741,891	" " " 1889.... 46,343,208
" " " 1890.... 24,402,093	" " " 1890.... 48,243,300
Union Pacific Co.	**Pennsylvania (Lines East of Pittsburg.)**
Gross Earnings for 1887....$28,557,766	Gross Earnings for 1887....$55,671,313
" " " 1888 ... 30,195,521	" " " 1888.... 58,172,077
" " " 1889... 31,070,182	" " " 1889.... 61,514,445
" " " 1890*... 41,871,813	" " " 1890.... 66,391,343
N. Y. Central & H. R. R. R. Co.	**Canadian Pacific Co.**
Gross Earnings for 1887....$36,296,024	Gross Earnings for 1887 ...$11,606,413
" " " 1888.... 35,283,584	" " " 1888.... 13,193,536
" " " 1889... 36,056,598	" " " 1889.... 15,030,660
" " " 1890.... 36,258,641	" " " 1890.... 16,540,088

*Increased mileage accounts for a part of the large Earnings of 1890.

This table shows that with one exception the earnings of the lines mentioned, and especially of the immediate rivals of the Canadian Pacific Co., have been and are steadily and rapidly increasing.

I beg leave to submit the following confirmatory article from *The Railway Age*, the leading railroad journal of this country under date of January 25, 1890, showing the effect upon the Northern Pacific Railway :

"The Northern Pacific Company at the commencement of the present year had about 3,725 miles of completed track owned and operated, and the addition of the Wisconsin Central lines make up the grand total of a little over 4,450 miles, forming a vast and far-reaching system, now extending from Lake Michigan to the Pacific Ocean, with main line and branches lying in the States of Illinois, Wisconsin, Minnesota, Dakota, Washington, and Oregon, and the Territories of Montana and Idaho. The Northern Pacific has, moreover, pushed northward into Manitoba, where, under the title of the Northern Pacific & Manitoba Railroad, it already has nearly 200 miles of lines in operation, with important extensions under way and contemplated. The company will also naturally continue the work of opening up new territory along its main lines by other extensions, so that it is evidently the question of but a short time when the mileage of the Northern Pacific system will have passed the 5,000-mile point, with possibilities of almost indefinite growth. Looking back only ten years, when the road consisted of only 530 miles of bankrupt line, ending at the Missouri River, and contrasting with that the vast mileage and prosperous condition of the company to-day, we have an impressive example of the changed conditions of this company and of many other railway properties which have arisen within comparatively so short a time. The Northern Pacific Company has fought its way from the depths of depression to a commanding position among the great railway systems of the land, and the remarkable increase in its earnings during the last year, when they reached the *grand total of 21,753,000 dollars*, gives its owners reason to hope for still better things."

The most bitter and determined rivals of the Grand Trunk Co. are the Lake Shore & Michigan Southern Co. and the Michigan Central Co. These two companies have, in their imagination, been almost bankrupted by the competition of the Grand Trunk Co. Poor's Manual for 1890, however, tells quite a different story. It shows that while the average annual gross earnings of the Lake Shore & Michigan Southern Co. from 1883 to 1889 inclusive, were $17,082,571; for 1890 they reached the sum of $20,874,200. That the average annual gross earnings of the Michigan Central Co. for the same period were $12,931,429, while for 1890 they reached $14,340,000. These figures do not seem to require any comment.

It has been testified before this committee that the Canadian Pacific Company is "the *alter ego* of the Dominion," "the Canadian government on wheels," "that it is dependent upon American traffic, without which it could not be successfully operated," and one very prominent witness, Mr. Henry V. Poor, declares "that its end, like that of the Intercolonial Railroad (which is owned and operated by the government), will be to become a burden on the Dominion treasury and create an annual deficit." The truth is that every one of its obligations to the Dominion Government has either been paid or absolutely provided for, so that the government is no more financially interested in the Canadian Pacific system to-day than is the government of the United States in the Pennsylvania system. The Canadian Pacific Railway is as purely a commercial enterprise as is the Pennsylvania Railway, and a marvelously successful one, as shown by the balance sheet for the year ending December 31st, 1889:

The gross earnings for the year were	$15,030,660 38
The working expenses were	9,024,601 04
The net earnings were	$6,006,059 34
Deduct the fixed charges accruing during the year	3,779,132 94
The surplus was	$2,226,926 40
Dividend of one per cent. paid February 17th, 1890	650,000 00
Leaving a surplus carried forward	$1,576,926 40
Surplus of previous year	326,423 92
Total surplus carried forward	$1,903,350 32

Of the above gross earnings of $15,030,660.38, American interstate traffic furnished $999,732.23, or 6.65 per cent. of the whole. Deduct operating expenses, say 66 per cent., and the net earnings *dependent upon American Interstate traffic* will be seen to cut a ridiculously small figure in the company's revenue.

The significance of these figures is greatly enhanced when we remember that the road was not completed to the Pacific coast until 1886, and the short line across the State of Maine was not completed until the mid-summer of 1889. Another remarkable fact in view of this balance sheet is shown by the statistics of railways for 1889, recently issued by the Inter-State Commerce Commission. On page 21 of this volume is a table showing revenue and density of traffic for all roads whose annual gross revenue exceeds $3,000,000, in which it appears that the Canadian Pacific Railway, with two exceptions, earns *the lowest gross revenue per mile of line of any of the seventy-eight roads with which it is compared.* The comparison, with the exceptions, is as follows: Canadian Pacific, $2,769; Missouri, Kansas & Texas, $2,704; Chicago, Kansas & Nebraska, $1,926.

How can the Canadian Pacific pay dividends and accumulate a surplus from such a small revenue? Its operating expenses in proportion to operating income is even greater than those of the leading rivals, as shown by the same volume of statistics, as follows: Canadian Pacific, *65.52 per cent.;* Northern Pacific, *60.37 per cent.;* Union Pacific, *56.51 per cent.* How, then, can the Canadian Pacific pay dividends and accumulate a surplus on such a small revenue? Because it was honestly built and is economically managed. Its stock has not been watered; no construction companies are gnawing its vitals, and the profits on every collateral enterprise connected with it, such as express, telegraph, elevators, hotels, restaurants, sleeping, dining and parlor cars, *all go into the treasury of the company for the benefit of its shareholders.* It presents in these respects a great object lesson to American railway managers.

The existence of the Canadian Pacific Railroad is asserted to be a military menace to the United States. On the contrary, it seems to me a military weakness so far as offensive operations against this country are concerned. A line of communication stretching along our border fifteen hundred miles, from Winnipeg to Vancouver, and largely over open prairies, could scarcely be defended by all the forces of the British Empire. Gen. Miles has testified before this committee that the United States Government would be able to take possession of this line within ten days from the outbreak of hostilities.

SEVENTH REASON.—PROTECTION TO AMERICAN INDUSTRY.

This reason was most plausibly stated to this Committee by Mr. A. N. Towne, vice-pres. of the Southern Pacific Railroad, who insists that the national policy is now settled, and should apply to railroads as well as to other forms of industry. I will not discuss the logical strength of the position, but I strongly suspect that such an application of the doctrine would detach so many Republican voters in the northeast, west and northwest as to endanger the further existence of the policy.

The utter inconsistency of Mr. Towne's practice with his theory cannot be better illustrated than to show the measure of protection given the American merchant and manufacturer by the Southern Pacific Railroad Co., as per the following table, which is taken from the findings in the opinion of the Interstate Commerce Commission recently rendered in the case of the *New York Board of Trade and Transportation et al. vs. The Pennsylvania R. R. Co. et al.* or the Import Rate case as before referred to. I subjoin also a portion of the opinion which holds that such rates are a direct violation of the law.

"The following table, compiled from data in the office of the Interstate Commerce Commission in regard to the tariff rates in evidence, shows through rates and divisions of through rates for the ocean and inland carriage on freights destined to the Pacific coast and imported from Liverpool through the Port of New Orleans; and also freight rates on domestic traffic:

Freight Rates in Cents per Hundred Pounds, to San Francisco, Sacramento, Marysville, Stockton, San Jose, Oakland (Sixteenth Street), and Los Angeles, Cal.

COMMODITIES.	From Liverpool, Eng. via New Orleans.			From New Orleans, La.	From New York, N. Y.	From Chicago, Ill.
	Ship's proportion.	Inland proportion.	Through.			
Agricultural Implements	19	70	89	114	130	119
Blacking	19	70	89	106	120	110
Books	27	80	107	264	300	275
Boots and Shoes	27	80	107	370	420	390
Burlaps	19	70	89	180	200	185
Buttons	27	80	107	374	420	390
Candles	19	70	89	125	150	130
Canned Fish	19	70	89	106	120	110
Carpets	27	80	107	288	330	300
Cashmeres	27	80	107			
Cement	19	70	89	106	120	110
Chinaware	27	80	107	163	190	170
Chocolate	27	80	107	125	150	130
Cigars	27	80	107	370	420	390
Clothing	27	80	107	374	420	390
Confectionery	27	80	107	187	215	195
Cordage	19	70	89	125	215	180
Crayons and Chalks	27	80	107	125	150	130
Crockery	19	70	89	125	150	180
Cutlery	27	80	107	326	370	340
Drugs, Common	19	70	89	187	215	195
Dry Goods	27	80	107	374	420	390
Earthenware	19	70	89	106	120	110
Feathers	27	80	107	374	420	390
Glassware, Common	19	70	89	125	150	130
Gloves	27	80	107			
Glycerine	27	80	107	106	120	110
Groceries, N. O. S.	19	70	89	370	420	390
Hair Goods	27	80	107			
Hardware	27	80	107	187	215	195
Hats and Caps	27	80	107	370	420	390
Hosiery	27	80	107	374	420	290
Lace	27	80	107			
Leather	27	80	107	326	370	340
Linen	27	80	107			
Linen Goods	27	80	107			
Milk, Condensed	19	70	89	106	120	110
Nails	19	70	89	106	120	110
Optical Goods	27	80	107			
Pins	27	80	107	264	300	275
Saddlers' Goods	27	80	107	370	420	390
Soap	19	70	89	106	120	110
Soda, Caustic, 2,480,162 lbs	19	70	89	106	120	110
Tallow	19	70	89	106	120	110
Woolen Goods	27	80	107			

"The road's import traffic is increasing and has about doubled, comparing 1885 with 1889. All this traffic went by sailing vessels and steamship lines via Panama until the Southern Pacific Company opened the New Orleans line. The claim of the company now is that not one-tenth of it is carried by its line, and that without the reduced through rate and the through line the road would get none of it."

" So far as Europe is concerned the Southern Pacific Company does not regard the Canada lines as being serious competitors with it. The Northern Pacific Railroad Company carries little, if any, of this particular traffic. The nine-tenths of the traffic not carried by the Southern Pacific Company, it is estimated, is carried by sailing vessels via Cape Horn and steamships via Panama."

" These circumstances and conditions are indeed widely different in many respects from the circumstances and conditions surrounding the carriage of domestic interstate traffic between the States of the American Union by rail carriers; but as the regulation provided for by the Act to Regulate Commerce does not undertake to regulate or govern them, they cannot be held to constitute reasons in themselves why imported freight brought to a port of entry of the United States or a port of entry of an adjacent foreign country destined to a place within the United States should be carried at a lower rate than domestic traffic from such ports of entry respectively to the places of destination in the United States over the same line and in the same direction. To hold otherwise would be for the Commission to create exceptions to the operation of the statute not found in the statute; and no other power but Congress can create such exceptions in the exercise of legislative authority."

" One paramount purpose of the Act to Regulate Commerce, manifest in all its provisions, is to give to all dealers and shippers the same rates for similar services rendered by the carrier in transporting similar freight over its line. Now, it is apparent from evidence in this case that many American manufacturers, dealers and localities, in almost every line of manufacture and business, are the competitors of foreign manufacturers, dealers and localities, for supplying the wants of the American consumers at interior places in the United States, and that under domestic bills of lading they seek to require from American carriers like service as their foreign competitors in order to place their manufactured goods, property and merchandise with interior consumers. The Act to Regulate Commerce secures them this right. To deprive them of it by any course of transportation business or device is to violate the Statute. Such a deprivation would be so obviously unjust as to shock the general sense of justice of all the people of the country except the few who would receive the immediate and direct benefit of it."

An examination of the long list of articles in this table

shows the freight on all of them with a single exception to be greater from New Orleans to San Francisco, than from Liverpool to San Francisco via New Orleans. The exception is glycerine, which pays 107 cents per 100 lbs. from Liverpool to San Francisco, and 106 cents per 100 lbs, from New Orleans to San Francisco. Upon the English shipment of this article the Southern Pacific Railroad (the balance going to the foreign steamship) receives 70 cents per 100 lbs. while upon the American shipment, the service being precisely the same in both cases, it receives 106 cents per 100 lbs., in other words, this patriotic Railroad company charges its American patrons *fifty-one per cent. more than it does its English patrons.* Upon all other articles the discrimination is still greater, requiring in the shipment of groceries, N. O. S. (not otherwise specified), *428 per cent. more freight money from the American than from the English shippers.* This vociferous advocate of protection against the competition of foreign railways, thus favors English at the expense of American interests.

I respectfully submit, therefore, that none of the seven alleged reasons for further legislative control of the Canadian railroads have any foundation in fact, and unless some better ones can be adduced, that the Congress of the United States ought not to be placed in the position of a quasi-side partner with any set of railroad corporations, in their purely business struggles with others for an increased traffic.

It should be borne in mind that no official of the Canadian railroads has ever claimed exemption from the Inter-State Commerce act of any traffic carried in connection with an American railroad, but on the contrary the General Manager of the Grand Trunk Company, Sir Joseph Hickson, and the President of the Canadian Pacific Company, Mr. W. C. Van Horne, both swore at the hearing in New York, in May, 1889, that they consider "that all traffic going over their lines in which American railroads participated, is subject to the Inter-State Commerce Act in all respects, and further that their tariffs covering such traffic were all on file with the Inter-State Commerce Commission as required by law, and were accessible for examination by anyone."

The Interstate Commerce Commission have held in the only two cases before it, in which the question of jurisdiction over Canadian railroads could be raised, that any traffic moving over a single foot of American territory, even though never out of the possession and control of the Canadian carrier and non-competitive with any American carrier, is nevertheless subject to the act. The Commission has thus asserted its jurisdiction over the carriage of coal from Buffalo to Canada, and over the carriage of Asiatic products from Yokohama via Vancouver to the United States, and to Canada, if touching American territory en route.

Thus far the Canadian railroads have cheerfully and promptly conformed to every suggestion and requirement of the Commission and *until they refuse on jurisdictional grounds* to be bound by the rules to which their American rivals submit, there can be no necessity for legislative action against them. The feeling in American commercial circles adverse to congressional action which would unnecessarily cripple the competition of Canadian with American railroads cannot be better expressed than in the reply to an interrogatory propounded to the Chicago Board of Trade by the Senate Committee on Interstate Commerce, in July, 1889. The interrogatory was: "Do you consider any additional legislation expedient or desirable for the regulation of the commerce carried on by railroad or water routes between the United States and Canada?" The reply was: "We do not consider any additional legislation necessary. The adoption of any legislative measures calculated to restrict the transportation facilities now enjoyed by the farmers, cotton growers and cattle raisers of the west and southwest, *would, in the opinion of this committee, bury in impenetrable oblivion, the political party that accomplished it.* The west would act as one man, and be aided and abetted by the independent voter of New England in the furtherance of such desirable obsequies."

I desire to say in passing that no complaint under the penal section of the act has ever been lodged against the Canadian railroads.

If my statements of fact and conclusions therefrom are well founded, there is no need to discuss at any length the questions of international jurisdiction and comity which must be involved in any attempt to control by Congressional action the purely local interstation traffic of Canada lying between points past which American bonded traffic is carried. Even if the jurisdictional objection should be waived by our Canadian neighbors, which is quite improbable, the configuration of Canadian territory is such, that a general application to its purely local traffic of the long and short haul clause of our law would be fraught with marked injustice. For example, the Canadian interstation traffic lying between Sault Ste. Marie, Port Huron, and Detroit on the west, and the St Lawrence and Niagara frontiers of the State of New York on the east, could not be expected to submit to restrictions from which the entire interstation traffic of the great States of New York, Pennsylvania, Illinois, and every other State is exempted by the very terms of the Interstate Commerce Act, which reads as follows :

"*Provided, however*, That the provisions of this act shall not apply to the transportation of passengers or property *wholly within one State* and not shipped to or from a foreign country from or to any State or Territory as aforesaid."

I will close these necessarily somewhat desultory remarks, with the consideration of one more statement made to this Committee by a prominent witness before referred to, which also the Interstate Commerce Commission have hastily indorsed. A very slight examination of the matter will demonstrate, beyond all controversy, the error into which both have fallen. I quote from page 897 of the testimony already printed by this Committee:

"*How the Dominion Government by Statutory Enactment Aids the Canadian Railroads in Competing with the Railroads of the United States.*

"While the Interstate Commerce Act of the United States operates as a restraint upon our railroads in their attempt to meet the competition of Canadian lines, the laws of Canada by special statutory exemption aid the railroads of that country in their persistent efforts to encroach upon American railroads. This fact is clearly set forth by the Interstate Commerce Commission in its recently published third annual report. Referring to the Canadian railroads the Commission says:

"They are practically under no restrictions imposed by their own statutes in respect to long and short haul traffic, but are at liberty to charge high rates on local business, to idemnify for losses on through or international business. Their managers deny with more or less emphasis that their local traffic is subjected to higher rates, but when the liberty to make such charges and the necessity for it co-exists, the inducement at least is strong. The provisions of the Canadian statute on this subject are as follows:

"SEC. 226. The company, in fixing or regulating the tolls to be demanded and taken for the transportation of goods shall, except in respect to through traffic to or from the United States, adopt and conform to any uniform classification of freight which the governor in council, on the report of the minister, from time to time prescribes.

"SEC. 232. No company, in fixing any toll or rate, shall, under like conditions and circumstances, make any unjust or partial discrimination between different localities ; but no discrimination between localities, which by reason of competition by water or railway, it is necessary to make to secure traffic, shall be deemed to be unjust or partial."

"These enactments give all traffic carried in competition with our carriers unlimited freedom."

"Mr. Chairman, these statutory provisions of the Dominion Government are part and parcel of a general line of political encroachment upon American interests."

I beg leave in this connection to submit the following sections from the Canadian Railway Act of 1888:

The Railway Committee.

SEC. 8. The Railway Committee of the Privy Council shall consist of the Minister of Railways and Canals, who shall be chairman thereof; of the Minister of Justice, and of two or more of the other members of the Queen's Privy Council for Canada, to be from time to time appointed by the Governor in Council, three of whom shall form a quorum; and such committee shall have the powers and perform the duties assigned to it by this act.

What matters Railway Committee may hear and determine.

SEC. 11. "The Railway Committe shall have power to inquire into, hear and determine any application, complaint or dispute respecting (among other things):

(*a*) Unjust preferences, discrimination or extortion;

(*b*) Any matter, act or thing which, by this or the special act is sanctioned, required to be done or prohibited.

Powers of inquiry, etc.

SEC. 13. The Railway Committee, the Minister, inspecting engineer, commissioner for inquiry into accident or casualty, or person appointed to make inquiry or report, may, among other things:

(*a*) Require the attendance of all such persons as it or he thinks fit to call before it or him and examine and require answers or returns to such inquiries as it or he thinks fit to make.

(*b*) Require the production of all books, papers, plans, specifications, drawings and documents relating to the matter before him.

Compelling attendance of witnesses, etc.

SEC. 15. The Railway Committee, the Minister and every such engineer, commissioner or person shall have the same power to enforce the attendance of witnesses and to compel them to give evidence and produce the books, papers or things, which they are required to produce, as is vested in any court in civil cases.

SEC. 17. Any decision or order made by the Railway committee under this act may be made an order of the

Exchequer court of Canada, or of any Superior court of any province of Canada, and shall be enforced in like manner as any rule of such court.

SEC. 214. The company may, subject to the provisions and restrictions in this and in the special act contained, make by-laws, rules or regulations for the following purposes, * * * * (various matters). *Company may make by-laws for certain purposes.*

SEC. 217. All such by-laws, rules and regulations shall be submitted from time to time to the Governor in Council for approval, and no such by-law, rule or regulation shall have any force or effect until it is approved by the Governor in Council.. *Sanction of by-laws.*

SEC. 223. Subject to the provisions and restrictions in this and in the special act contained, the company may, by by-laws, or the directors if thereunto authorized by the by-laws may, from time to time fix and regulate the tolls to be demanded and taken for all passengers and goods transported upon the railway or in steam vessels belonging to the company. *Tolls, how fixed.*

SEC. 224. Such tolls may be fixed either for the whole or for any particular portions of the railway ; but all such tolls shall always under the same circumstances, be charged equally to all persons, and at the same rate, whether per ton, per mile or otherwise, in respect of all passengers and goods and railway carriages of the same description, and conveyed or propelled by a like railway carriage or engine, passing only over the same portion of the line of railway ; and no reduction or advance in any such tolls shall be made either directly or indirectly, in favor of or against any particular company or person traveling upon or using the railway. *No discrimination to be made.*

SEC. 225. The tolls fixed for large quantities or long distances may be proportionately less than the tolls fixed for small quantities or short distances, if such tolls are, under the same circumstances charged equally to all persons ; but in respect of quantity no special toll or rate shall be given *Special rates.*

or fixed for any quantity less than one car load of at least ten tons.

Classification of freight.
Sec. 226. The company in fixing or regulating the tolls to be demanded and taken for the transportation of goods, shall, except in respect to through traffic to or from the United States, *adopt and conform to any uniform classification of freight* which the Governor in Council on the report of the minister from time to time, prescribes.

Tolls to be approved by Governor in Council.
Sec. 227. No tolls shall be levied or taken until the by-law fixing such tolls has been approved of by the Governor in Council, nor until after two weekly publications in the Canada Gazette of such by-law and of the order in council approving thereof; nor shall any company levy or collect any money for services as a common carrier except subject to the provisions of this act.

Revision of by-law fixing tolls.
Sec. 228. Every by-law fixing and regulating tolls shall be subject to revision by the Governor in Council, from time to time, after approval thereof.

Tariffs to be posted up.
Sec. 230. The company shall from time to time cause to be printed and posted up in its offices, and in every place where the tolls are to be collected, in some conspicuous position, a printed board or paper exhibiting all the rates of tolls payable, and particularizing the price or sum of money to be charged or taken for the carriage of any matter or thing.

Discrimination when allowable.
Sec. 232. No company, in fixing any toll or rate, shall, under the conditions and circumstances, make any unjust or partial discrimination between different localities; but no discrimination between localities which, by reason of competition by water or railway, it is necessary to make to secure traffic, shall be deemed unjust or partial.

No secret special rates to be given.
Sec. 233. No company shall make or give any secret special toll, rate, rebate, drawback or concession, to any person; and every company shall, on the demand of any

person, make known to him any special rate, rebate, drawback or concession, given to any one.

SEC. 240. Every company shall, according to its power, afford all reasonable facilities to any other railway company for the receiving and forwarding and delivery of traffic upon and from the several railways belonging to or worked by such companies respectively, and for the return of carriages, trucks and other vehicles ; and no such company shall make or give any undue or unreasonable preference or advantage to or in favor of any particular person or company, or any particular description of traffic in any respect whatsoever,—nor shall any such company subject any particular person or company, or any particular description of traffic to any undue or unreasonable prejudice or disadvantage in any respect whatsoever ; and every company which has or works a railway which forms part of a continuous line of railway, or which intersects any other railway, or which has any terminus, station or wharf near to any terminus, station or wharf of any other railway, shall afford all due and reasonable facilities for receiving and forwarding by its railway all the traffic arriving by such other railway, without any unreasonable delay, and without any such preference or advantage or prejudice or disadvantage, as aforesaid, and so that no obstruction is offered to the public desirous of using such railway as a continuous line of communication, and so that all reasonable accommodation, by means of the railways of the several companies, is at all times afforded to the public in that behalf ; and any agreement made between any two or more companies contrary to this section shall be unlawful and null and void.

Facilities to be afforded in respect to traffic.

No undue advantage.

Agreements in violation to be void.

SEC. 241. Every officer, servant or agent of any company, having the superintendence of the traffic at any station or depot thereof, who refuses or neglects to receive, convey or deliver at any station or depot of the company for which they are destined, any passenger, goods or thing, brought,

Penalty for refusal to receive and convey goods.

conveyed or delivered to him or such company for conveyance over or along its railway from that of any other company, intersecting or being near to such first mentioned railway, or who in any way willfully violates the provisions of the next preceding section, and the company first mentioned, are, for each refusal, neglect or offense severally liable in summary conviction, to a penalty not exceeding fifty dollars over and above the actual damages sustained; which penalty shall be recoverable with costs, by the railway company or by any such person aggrieved by such neglect or refusal, and such penalty shall belong to the said railway company, or other person so aggrieved.

Recovery and application.

SEC. 242. Every company which grants any facilities to any incorporated express company or person shall grant equal facilities on equal terms and conditions to any other incorporated express company which demands the same.

Equal facilities to express co.'s, etc.

SEC. 289. Every company, director or officer doing, causing or permitting to be done any matter, act or thing contrary to the provisions of this or the special act, or to the orders or directions of the Governor in Council, or of the railway committee, or minister made hereunder, or omitting to do any matter, act or thing, required to be done on the part of any such company, director or officer, is liable to any person injured thereby for the full amount of damages sustained by such act or omission; and if no other penalty is in this or the special act provided for any such act or omission, is liable for each offense, to a penalty of not less than twenty dollars, and not more than five thousand dollars, in the discretion of the court before which the same is recoverable.

Liability of company, etc., in cases specified.

Penalty.

SEC. 2. This section shall only apply to companies and directors and officers of companies within the legislative authority of the parliament of Canada.

SEC. 290. Every person from whom any company exacts any unjust or extortionate toll, rate or charge shall, in addi-

Damages for extortionate tolls.

tion to the amount so unjustly exacted, be entitled to recover from the company as damages an amount equal to three times the amount so unjustly exacted.

A careful examination of these provisions of the Canadian Railroad Act, some of them, notably section 240, being almost identical in terms with our own, discloses that Canadian railroads are substantially as closely restricted by law in their dealings with Canadian merchants and shippers as are our own in dealing with American merchants and shippers. In one respect at least their system is superior to our own, in that the orders of their tribunal, the Railway Committee, are given the force of orders of court, while our tribunal, the Interstate Commerce Commission, has no legal power to enforce its decrees. It is therefore idle to suppose that Canadian railroads, with such prompt and efficient remedies in the hands of their patrons, can long subject them to unjust charges as compared with those placed upon international traffic.

The charges imposed upon any article of freight carried by any railroad, whether American or Canadian, depends upon the class of articles to which it belongs. Freight generally, is divided on most American roads into ten classes. This basis of division is not however, universally observed. In some sections of our country a larger number of classes are used, in others a smaller number. Even where the same *number* of classes are used, it not unfrequently happens that an article rated as 5th class in one section of our country, may for illustration, be rated in another section as 3d class or 7th class. This has given rise to various systems of classification, known as the Trunk Line Classification, Middle States Classification, Western States Classification and Southern Railway and Steamship Classification.

It will be noted that the Canadian roads are by law obliged to submit their *local* classification to the Governor in Council for approval, hence this classification which differs in some respects from any used by American roads, is known among railroad men as the Canadian Official Classification." It is evident that if Canadian railroads participate in the carriage of American traffic they must also participate in the classification under which that traffic is carried. In order, therefore, to enable them to conform to the classifications of their American connections, and at the same time avoid a violation of Canadian law, section 226 provides that "through traffic to or from the United States" may be excepted from the official classification which the Governor in Council from time to time prescribes. *Instead then of section 226 being a menace to American traffic, or American railroads, it is a voluntary concession to both.*

In section 232, the "localities" between which discrimination may under certain circumstances be exercised, are assuredly only those over which Canadian jurisdiction extends, and therefore cannot be "localities" in the United States, and the wildest stretch of imagination cannot torture the clause into meaning a privilege of discrimination between a "locality" in Canada and a "locality" in the United States. The traffic affected by this section being then local Canadian traffic which perforce *cannot* be carried by American carriers, and therefore cannot be carried in *competition* with them ; there can be no justification for the statement above quoted, "these enactments give all traffic carried in competition with our carriers unlimited freedom." Besides it has been held by the Interstate Commerce Commission that an American railroad "competing with water or with a foreign railway for traffic important in amount and controlling in effect, may be relieved from the long and short haul clause of the act." The Commission has further held that Interstate traffic between two points, competitive with local State traffic between the same two points, may also be relieved from the long and short haul clause of the act. This is a complete acknowledgment of the soundness of the principle of the Canadian law, and should forever stop any further denunciation of it, as a menace to the United States.

www.ingramcontent.com/pod-product-compliance
Lightning Source LLC
Chambersburg PA
CBHW020730100426
42735CB00038B/1502